# Wild
## with a glue gun

*"I love that I have found support from this group through many different stages of my life. In addition to great craft ideas I have gotten advice on hormones, teenagers, balancing a frantic life ..."*
—Cynthia

*"Our group is a great place to get feedback or ideas for projects that aren't working out as expected. There is always someone who can recommend the best paint, or knitting store, or quilt repair technique."*
—Lisa

# Wild with a Glue Gun

GETTING TOGETHER WITH CRAFTY FRIENDS

• INCLUDES 65 CREATIVE PROJECTS •

Kitty Harmon
and Christine Stickler

NORTH LIGHT BOOKS
Cincinnati, Ohio

For two inspired mothers:
Phyl, who taught by example,
and Patricia, a nurturer of craftiness

08 07 06 05 04    5 4 3 2 1

**Library of Congress Cataloging-in-Publication Data**

Harmon, Kitty
   Wild with a glue gun : getting together with crafty friends : includes 65 creative projects / Kitty Harmon and Christine Stickler.
     p. cm.
    ISBN 1-58180-472-5 (pbk. : alk. paper)
    1. Paper work. I. Stickler, Christine. II. Title.

   TT870.H34 2004
   745.5—dc22

               2003059286

Acknowledgments listed in full on page 143.
Credits on page 143 constitute an extension of this copyright page.

Book design by Jane Jeszeck, Jigsaw, Seattle
Photography by Jim Fagiolo except as noted (see page 143)
Photo styling by Lisa Crabtree and Jane Jeszeck
Copyediting by Alice Marsh

# Contents

## FORMING A CRAFT GROUP

# Introduction

The results of an important medical study have just been released. Researchers studied three groups: one, a group of friends who made crafts together; another, a group of women who didn't know each other previously but also met regularly to do crafts; and a control group of women who did not engage in any group crafting. The researchers checked in with their sub-jects every five years or so, and at the end of twenty years, put their subjects through a series of rigorous tests. The results were conclusive and startling.

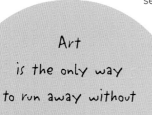

The women in the first group were healthy specimens with perfect blood pressure readings, strong hearts, no signs of dementia and lustrous skin and nails. They also were extremely well-informed, spoke in complex sentences and shared a highly evolved sense of humor. The second group had nearly identi-cal results with the exception that stress levels ran higher, possibly due to a rumor circulated among them that the head researcher was really Martha Stewart in disguise.

> Art
> is the only way
> to run away without
> leaving home.
> —Twyla Tharp

The last group, as you might imagine, did not fare well, at least those who were still living, that is. Don't worry; they're forming a craft group of their own. Though the study is over, the members of the other groups still meet regularly and plan to for the rest of their long, healthy lives.

OK, so all of the above is bunk. But anyone who ever has enjoyed an hour of relaxing with friends while making something—anything—with her hands knows that such a study is not necessary. It's obvious that it's good for you. It's a simple equation: time with friends + time spent creating = sanity.

Perhaps we can divide the world into two groups of people. There are those who get cranky if they miss regular creativity sessions. Then there are the others. They aren't craft-inclined and may make sarcastic remarks about beads and yarn and little pots of paint. Yet we know that creating something from raw mate-rials such as these is like manna to crafty beings.

Our experience started eleven years ago with the formation of Christine's group, Women Who Do Things with Their Hands. That group inspired Kitty and friends to gather around the art table; they call themselves Women Who Run with Glue Guns. Together we are twenty-three women living in the Seattle area, most of whom contributed to this book in some way. We range in age from 29 to 58; we're single and married, career slaves and stay-at-home moms, democrats and republicans, Christians and atheists. And we all get along! Now if only the world's leaders would sit down and make crafts together.

The projects we engage in as a group do not have pretensions to art, though the results may well be highly artistic. Rather, this is creativity that engages the hands and leaves the mind free to travel wherever it wants to go. In medical settings they call this therapy, and we do, too. There's a calming magic about manual creativity; as the hands cut and glue, draw and paint, arrange and design, the mind quiets down, even purrs. One friend calls this "the drool zone." The cares of the day recede and the world shrinks down to a manageable size, the area immediately in front of you.

> Creativity is a drug I cannot live without.
> —Cecil B. DeMille

So, have we convinced you to form your own craft group? Because, believe us, the camaraderie of artistic companions is the best soul food available. Call it a throwback to the old quilting circles or our mothers' "stitch-and-bitch" groups. Call it multi-tasking or mixing pleasure with pleasure. It's a winning formula: a chance to get together with other imaginative individuals for mutual inspiration. Food, wine, laughter and a good project ... it just doesn't get much better.

The beauty of being part of a craft club is that you will make time in your life on a regular basis for making things. It will spur you to get those unfinished projects out of the drawer. Your friends will admire what you're doing, and you'll want to do more. It seems that the more creative you are, the more creative you'll want to be. Our book will encourage you down that path.

As a fellow inventive being, we hope you'll understand and appreciate our unique approach in this book. We don't waste pages telling you how to gather a group of friends for crafting time. (Just put out the word and they will come!) There are no photographs of anonymous models' torsos with clean aprons and well-manicured hands, and there are no tips for making storage boxes for lace or correctly addressing a wedding invitation. We assume that your ingenious spirit wants the freedom to approach any given project its own way and that achieving someone else's idea of perfection is not the goal. We simply provide projects we've enjoyed making and the things we've learned along the way and hope that you will take these ideas to glorious new heights of creativity.

We do offer you the stories of our own groups and those of others we know. Of course, there are count-less ways to structure such a group, but we've found that our flexible models have worked well for us, so we share them with you. Then we present a range of projects you can tackle more or less in one sitting. Each project has an ambition scale that takes into account the quantity of materials and ease of getting them; the knowledge, skills or talent the project requires and the concentration you'll have to muster.

> Creative minds have always been known to survive any kind of bad training.
> —Anna Freud

This book aims to inspire you to do whatever it takes to give yourself time and space for regular bouts of creativity. Who knows where it'll take you and your crafty cohorts? Our experiences promise that you'll get more out of it than you expect. And if you don't do it for yourself, well, don't say we didn't warn you of the astonishing results of that medical study and the fate of the control group.

# Ten ways to make a craft group thrive

**❶ Gather a diverse group.** Invite members who don't all know each other and who differ in age and background.

**❷ Decide on an organizational format.** How many members do you want? Will you meet in the evening? How often? Do the members of your group want to work on their own projects, on one project led by a group member or some combination thereof? How will you decide when and how to add new members? Read the three group profiles that follow and decide which appeals to you most, or develop a new format of your own.

**❸ Remain flexible.** Follow one organizational format long enough for all members to decide if they like it, and if not, adapt it. Make a point of checking in once a year to gather members' input. Change is good.

**❹ Share the leadership.** Let everyone feel ownership of the group as much as possible so those who formed it don't shoulder all of the organizational burden and so others feel free to shape it. **Or don't share the leadership.** Some groups work better if one or two or three people take the lead. Often, some don't mind being the organizers if they can dictate what the group will be. What matters is that expectations are made clear from the start.

**❺ Invite guest experts.** On occasion, bring in a pro to demonstrate projects and teach new techniques. This can rev up a group's creative energies.

**❻ Don't let food become a focus.** If providing elaborate meals is a burden for the members or takes too much time from crafting, you will end up with a dinner club, not a craft group.

**❼ Celebrate.** Make gifts, as a group, to commemorate milestones in members' lives. It's fun to collaborate on a project now and then and more so to receive a handmade creation celebrating a marriage, baby, big birthday, parting or personal triumph.

**❽ Form traditions.** Reserve at least one gathering each year for an activity you all enjoy. Ideas: Take a field trip to an art museum, a pottery studio or a bead shop. Take an annual getaway weekend or a creative retreat. Issue a glue guns challenge: Give each member an object they must transform and bring to the next meeting. Award a Golden Glue Gun annually to the Gal Most Likely to Become Unglued. Anything that builds camaraderie and recognizes that another year in the life of your group is passing.

**❾ Take photos.** Years later, you'll be glad you documented the faces and the creations that have played a part in the life of your group.

**❿ Give back.** Be a generous group. Devote a gathering to making something to donate to a charity auction, for example. Adopt a women's craft collective in a developing country (see page 20). Encourage others. Inevitably, once you form a successful group, others will want to follow your lead; offer advice and project ideas to get them going.

# Group profiles

## Christine: Women Who Do Things with Their Hands

On a spring day about fifteen years ago, I sat watching my brother, a fisherman, mending fishing nets with his crew. They were sitting in a circle down at the docks, and as their hands wove through the nets, they entertained each other with stories. These men had a history together and a closeness that was powerful. No doubt many days at sea and their shared experiences had cemented their friendships, but something about their hands in motion, fingers working together, made them at ease with each other in a different way. I wanted to have this experience, too, with my women friends.

*"This group has what I call 'emotional intelligence.' We are careful with one another's feelings, very gentle, always encouraging."*

*—Florence*

As the mother of two and a full-time professional, there are relatively few tranquil moments in my life. Friendships mean a great deal to me, but connecting over lunch or a drink after work always feels rushed and not as meaningful as I'd like. I began thinking about a new idea: getting together with friends in a way that would be both stimulating and relaxing and would give us experiences to share. Our hands would be busy, engaged in creative projects, yet we would be

free to talk and deepen our friendships. Now, fourteen years later, the weekday evening or weekend afternoon when I meet with my friends, "Women Who Do Things with Their Hands," remains the one time each month I can count on for an oasis of stress-free creativity and conversation.

It's funny that it wasn't until my mid-thirties that I came up with this notion of connecting with others who shared my passion for "arts and crafts." I've always been drawn to making things with my hands. My Catholic schooling offered art activities that revolved around not much more than coloring photocopies of the saints, so I seized on any opportunity to do extra-credit projects that involved creative handiwork.

In college I took art classes, though it was clear I was no artistic genius, just so I could be involved in the creative process that so enthralled me. Once I had children, I became known as "the mom with all the fun art projects." I have always devoted an area of my house to materials for last-minute creative endeavors. It is apparent to all that I enjoy these activities as much, if not more, than the children who take part!

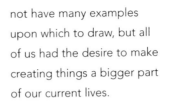

"The group has made me more unselfish. When I first started coming I would think in terms of "these are my things" and now the idea of sharing all that we have with one another is natural ... it has spilled over into my life elsewhere as well."
—Sarah

So in December of 1990, I invited twelve women to my house with an invitation that said simply: "Please come if you are interested in meeting monthly with a group of women who enjoy making things." We were a group with diverse backgrounds, family histories and perceptions of ourselves as "artists."

At that first meeting we talked about women in our families who were involved in making things with their hands. Many did

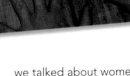

not have many examples upon which to draw, but all of us had the desire to make creating things a bigger part of our current lives.

The ground rules were simple. We would meet monthly and each of us would bring a project we were working on. In those first months, the projects varied from specific crafts, such as knitting, quilting and beadwork, to tasks like writing birth announcement cards or rewriting address books. In fact, we recently marked the beginning of our second decade by noting that Florence was redoing her address book for the second time! We all agreed that, in our full and frantic lives, the last thing we needed was another meeting that came with obligations and pressures. So if someone didn't come with a project, she was free to watch and converse or join in with what someone else was doing. We met on weekday evenings after dinner and usually stayed together for a few hours. Sometimes the host of the gathering would have a project to share, but participation was always optional.

"What is better than a table filled with art materials and everyone engaged in making and talking? It seems as if there are no boundaries to what can be created or discussed. It all flows."
—Charlotte

After our first year, we decided that we needed a weekend away where we could really focus on our projects and have fun together. We spent our first

getaway in a converted slaughter-house on a farm on Orcas Island. We stayed up almost all night creating projects with materials strewn throughout the building and guarding each other as we made runs to the outhouse while trying to dodge the rams fiercely protecting it. Since then, WWDTWTH have made annual visits to a variety of nearby island and beach retreats with carloads of projects and activities. Florence, who is from Haiti, introduced us to "grasse matinee," or fat morning, an entire day when you never get out of your pajamas. We quickly adopted this as the formula for our weekends. These have become treasured respites for all of us. We pack an amazing amount of creativity, laughter, good food, great conversations and walks in our PJs into these hours away.

In the last few years, we have added new members and new traditions. One was a switch to occasional Saturday morning meetings instead of our traditional weeknight time. One of the first times we did this was when Sarah, a wonderful ceramic artist in our group, invited us to a "mosaic madness afternoon," with directions to bring something to mosaic on or in—a flower pot, pizza box or cake pans—and odds and ends to mosaic with—beach glass, pebbles and so on.

*"This group has provided me with a circle of woman friends that are very unlike the corporate stereotypes I meet through my work world. They are strong, supportive and wildly creative."*

—*Kay*

She provided concrete, pottery shards, hammers, tile nippers and miscellaneous mosaic materials. And from this first gathering an annual "mosaic madness" event has evolved.

The size of the group has fluctuated. We now have a strong nucleus of twelve, six of whom were in the original group. Each year, we sit down and develop a schedule a year in advance that includes a combination of weeknight and Saturday meetings, one getaway weekend and a December holiday event.

We have been there for one another through all sorts of life events—births, marriages and deaths. The group has become an anchor in all of our lives. It doesn't take much imagination to see the group of us twenty, thirty or forty years down the road: still meeting, laughing and sharing our latest creations.

# Kitty: Women Who Run with Glue Guns

Last night's was a fairly typical Glue Guns gathering. We were outside in the garden behind Beth's house on a lovely summer evening near the solstice when it stays light until almost ten o'clock in Seattle. Plenty of time for catching up with each other, working on our various projects and—oh yes—eating. Food is not supposed to be the focus of our gatherings, but we always enjoy it along with plenty of wine. Especially at Beth's. We joke—gratefully, groaningly—about the gatherings at her house as being the most fattening of the year. Beth runs a catering business and makes a delicious salad and an unbelievable five-cheese macaroni-and-cheese, followed by Kahlua milkshakes for dessert. Somehow we still manage to get some crafting done.

Over the course of four or so hours last night we talked about a play that was just opening, Anne's new baby, a fossil-hunting trip some others are organizing, summer vacation plans, borrowing a road bike for a triathlon, a son's high school graduation, a local political scandal, good books, good movies and at least several dozen other topics. Meanwhile, Dana worked on her hooked rug, Lisa collaged a light switch cover, Julie made a bulletin board out of wine corks, Robyn wired copper-and-sea-glass creations for her garden, Lea knit a baby cap, Margaret made a collage, Anne

*"I'm a 47-year-old with an active professional and family life. I'm not afraid to admit it: I love to craft. Crafting not only is an outlet for my private whimsical and imaginative energy, it's also the bonding element in a community of friends, who share this activity as a form of creative expression."*

*—Margaret*

fashioned some candleholders out of old jars, and Pamela worked on a lamp she was donating to an auction. I played around with a new painting technique. Maryann ended up just relaxing and yacking.

We didn't all know each other at first, and even now that we do, most of us don't see each other often outside of the group. Two friends, Lynn and Lisa, helped me get the group started as an amalgam of our friends, and Lisa's husband came up with our name, which immediately stuck.

We've been meeting for about six years (no one can remember for sure when we started). Our membership has changed over time, but a good many of the original members are still with us. Several have moved away, but others are always waiting in the wings to take their places.

I say "member" and "places," but that implies a level of formality we've never really had. For about five years we had barely any structure at all. Christine got us going by sharing the ways that Women Who Do Things with Their Hands do things, but we never got around to doing a schedule of gatherings. At any given meeting someone in our group would offer to host the next one and would send an e-mail reminder a couple of weeks in advance. Everyone brought a dish of food or a bottle of wine and her own project. At Christmas we all make the same things, usually a gift like bath salts or vinegars to give to others, and hold a white elephant gift exchange.

dilemma": Do you join a book group because you want to read books you wouldn't otherwise read? Or would you resent having to read a book you didn't choose when there are so many other books stacked on your night table? We felt that with our busy schedules, working on our own projects made the most sense, plus the added benefit of seeing and learning from others' projects. More recently, the person hosting has provided an idea and extra materials for anyone who'd rather just show up and be given something to do, and that has been nice, too.

This arrangement worked fine for a while. Then, about a year ago, we decided to get a bit more organized. Now, whoever is hosting provides food and beverages with the help of an assigned partner (some would rather not host Glue Guns gatherings, most for lack of a big table, and so they are assigned as co-hosts). Even with an established schedule, we're always moving the dates around, but we are assured of meeting ten times a year, which is just right for us. We also adopted our first real rule, which is that we will never invite the current girlfriend of any member's ex-boyfriend. Believe it or not, this has come up.

*"We're not Martha Stewart wannabes. We could care less about doing things the proper way. We drink too much wine and have too much fun for that."*

*—Julie*

Everyone in our group of twelve or so has a fairly demanding work life: About half of us own our own businesses, and the other half hold challenging jobs. We decided to bring projects instead of providing them for the group because everyone is individually creative and no one seems to have the time to finish even her own projects. When getting started, we talked about the "book group

Whenever someone has a baby or moves away, we devote a meeting to making something as a group to give to that member. When Lynn moved to New York, we painted a floor cloth with aspects of the Pacific Northwest that we hoped would lure her back. When Anne had a baby, we made her a mobile of felt faces. Before Lynn had her baby, she flew back for a gathering, and we painted blocks with bright colors and used them to build bookends. One Christmas we gave kitchen counter facials and put henna designs on our hands.

Even if we were to switch to a format in which we all did the same project, some practices would not change. Lea, a prodigious knitter, hates to sew and

won't make anything that involves needle and thread. Lisa is a lapsed artist and sometimes makes Real Art on the spot. Margaret, a publications editor for most of her grown life, would rather spend her time cutting publications into little pieces than anything else. Beth likes to Get Things Done, usually wacky ideas that turn out great, like spray painting the cushions for her garden furniture. And at every meeting Maryann and Julie both maintain a pretense of tackling a project (usually organizing photo albums), but they love to talk even more, which keeps us all entertained.

You may wonder, where do the husbands and children go when we're meeting? They make themselves scarce, one way or another. They're not banished; they just don't tend to stick around. How do we decide whether to include, or not to include, family in some gatherings? We've discussed this question, and while some in our group would like to spend time getting to know spouses and children of women who have become friends, others (who have prevailed) feel strongly that these gatherings are our time, and we can organize events outside of Glue Guns gatherings for family socializing. A few others agree that their husbands have no interest in coming.

That's about it. The key to our success? We don't take ourselves too seriously. We laugh to think of ourselves as belonging to some kind of "serious" craft group. In fact, we laugh at the word "craft." We're not devoted enough. We just like to make things and enjoy good company while we're at it.

## Crafty Women

Trilby and Allison formed a craft group in 1994—as yet another spin-off from Women Who Do Things with Their Hands—that has been going strong ever since. Theirs provides yet another model of how to organize craft groups.

Early on, the members of Crafty Women discovered that when a craft project was announced in advance and materials provided, more people attended. In the beginning, they'd invite an "expert" to come and present a particular project every so often, but the arrangement evolved so that one

group member now takes responsibility for bringing a craft project, with all necessary materials, to each gathering. Members pitch in no more than five dollars apiece to defray expenses. Leftover supplies go into a joint crate that lives in the trunk of Allison's car and appears at each scheduled evening.

Crafty Women (eight to ten total, over the years) meet ten times a year, plus an August meeting just for planning. At this gathering everyone brings samples or pictures of things they'd like to make, and everyone votes for her top four choices. The winning

projects are parceled out among the members, though they usually are assigned to those who suggested them. After this planning meeting, Trilby prepares a flyer and sends it to all members. December is reserved for a cookie exchange and a quick Christmas craft, and January is devoted to making valentines. Members sign up to host and provide snacks on a given month. Trilby and Allison remain the prime movers of the group; they believe that you need organizers to make this model work, as someone has to prod members to initiate group projects and and gather materials.

The members of Crafty Women appreciate being able to show up and have something to make without having to plan for it in advance (those not hosting, that is). Alison comments that otherwise, she'd always be bringing her quilting or photo albums, projects that are too bulky for transporting and take up too much room at the table. Of the shared-project format, she says, "It's so interesting to see how differently our individual creativity surfaces. Someone will think of a particular way of doing a craft that turns out beautifully and never would have occurred to me, or vice versa. I love seeing the imaginative power that we sometimes don't even know we have." Trilby agrees. "It's funny—I really don't like having a lot of little

*"I'm a frustrated artist, and I find it so nice to have a way to make non-threatening projects on a regular basis without announcing to the world, 'Look at me! I'm making art!' This is just fun, and it's done in an evening, and with excellent company. It's just about perfect."*

—*Trilby*

things I've made cluttering up my home. That's just me. So why have I been in this group for nine years? I guess because it's so satisfying to make things. It's doing it, the process more than the end result, that I love."

The group's members are single women and women who are married without children, married with young children and married with grown children. Members range in age from early thirties to early fifties. "It's good that we are at different places in life," says Trilby. "It doesn't turn into a mommy club, and we can talk about nursing or menopause and there's always someone to chime in."

They like to keep their group to no more than ten women because, ideally, they want everyone to fit around a table. Out of ten on the roster, a manageable six usually show up. Adding new people to the group is an informal process, with members inviting friends on occasion. Some people are a perfect fit right away; others "just drop away," says Allison. "We don't ever worry about not having enough. People who hear about our group think it's a great idea. There is no shortage of women interested in getting together with like-minded crafty women."

# Women uniting in creativity: a worldwide tradition

You can bet that if Eve had had a few friends in Eden, she would have been busy making things with them instead of listening to that snake. Since the beginning of mankind, we imagine, there has always been a circle of women busy with their hands, making things to share with others. As a member of a craft group, you will be spinning a thread of tradition connecting you to quilting bees in post-Revolution America, Hmong women creating pa ndau story cloths, arpillera collectives in Peru, a women's trade union in Gujarat embroidering with mirrors and on and on, through history and around the globe. And that's just needlework!

It is inspiring to think of ourselves joining a long line of women from all parts of the world who find sustenance in one form or another from making things with our hands. For a beautiful testament to women's creativity around the world, treat yourself to a copy of *In Her Hands: Craftswomen Changing the World* by Paola Gianturco and Toby Tuttle.

You can make an even more direct connection between your group and those in far-flung places. Educate yourself about the growing number of international organizations working to support women's initiatives, specifically developing their own small businesses selling handmade crafts. Here is a selection of organizations involved in this movement. We were surprised to learn that few groups serve women artisans only, but all of the organizations we list do support women artisans' initiatives as at least part of what they do. We urge you

*Durban, South Africa: Zulu women from the National Multi-Skills Development Association gather grass to weave into mats.*

to go to their sites, learn more about their efforts, support these organizations by buying gifts from their catalogs and stores and tell your friends about them. You will be helping to keep the craft tradition alive and helping to empower women to rise out of poverty.

### Fair Trade Federation (FTF)
### www.fairtradefederation.org

FTF is an association of fair trade wholesalers, retailers and producers of products from around the world. Members are committed to providing fair wages and good employment opportunities to economically disadvantaged artisans and farmers. FTF directly links low-income producers with consumer markets and educates consumers about the importance of purchasing fairly traded products that support living wages and safe and healthy conditions for workers in the developing world. Now you can start asking before you buy: "Are you a member of FTF?"

### Tribal Fibers
### www.tribalfiber.com

Featured products are made by village cooperatives in northern Thailand.

*Pokhara, Nepal: Women's Skill Development Centre (Oxfam Australia Trading)*

## Aid to Artisans

www.aid2artisans.org

ATA offers practical assistance to artisans worldwide to foster artistic traditions and community-based economic growth. ATA's work includes revitalizing dormant craft traditions, strengthening local production capacity, introducing innovative new product designs and serving as a resource for commercial buyers.

## El Quetzal

www.elquetzal.org

This volunteer-run organizations sells cotton clothing and goods of Mayan design woven by Guatemalan women, with all proceeds going back to their communities. (Read the full story on page 20.)

## Global Exchange

www.globalexchange.org

Global Exchange offers unique gifts from around the world and educational resources about human rights issues. Artisans create handicrafts from beautiful traditional designs that have been passed down through families for centuries, and farming cooperatives produce fair-trade coffees, teas and chocolates.

## Mama Africa

www.mamaafrika.com

When you purchase gifts here, you support artisans, many of whom live solely from the income they earn selling their wares. Your purchases will also support the organizations working to promote these artisans. The site donates a portion of the proceeds from each order to a local cause.

JUDITH HADEN

*Gujarat, India: members of a women's embroidery cooperative (Oxfam Australia Trading)*

## Oxfam Community Aid Abroad

www.oxfamtrading.org.au

Oxfam Australia Trading promotes craft producers in developing areas in Asia, India, Africa and Latin America. They assist a variety of organizations, many specifically devoted to women, in promoting self-reliant trade and making products available to greater numbers of people. You can purchase products directly from the site or from any of seventeen stores if you happen to visit Australia.

## PEOPLink

www.catgen.com/partner

PEOPLink is a resource for artisans that offers training and tools for building a Web presence for their products so artisans can sell their items to anyone with Internet access. The database currently provides catalogs for 135 trading partners, of whom they estimate 80 percent are women.

## Ten Thousand Villages

www.tenthousandvillages.org

Ten Thousand Villages operates 180 retail stores across North America, providing fairly traded handicrafts from more than 110 artisan groups in Africa, Asia and Latin America. The stores are wonderful (we love the Seattle location), filled with baskets, jewelry, textiles, musical instruments and items for the home from more than thirty countries.

## How one craft group supports a Guatemalan weaving collective

Emily Arfin has been a member of a Seattle craft group for fifteen years. Making things is an important part of her life, as is activism for a variety of causes. During a visit to Guatemala, she was moved by the contrast between the lovely crafts of the Mayan people and their poverty and second-class status in a country where they are the majority. In 1997, Emily found a way to combine her love for craft-making with a desire to help the Maya. She joined the board of El Quetzal, a nonprofit organization based in Seattle whose mission is to help Mayan women move from political struggle to sustainable economic development.

El Quetzal is an economic development project that uses the resources of its Seattle organizers to provide access to markets for the artensanias (crafts) created in rural Guatemalan communities. The group focuses on Mayan women—the poorest, least educated sector of Guatemalan society—to help them preserve their backstrap weaving techniques and work in a way that also preserves their culture. After a process of interviews with several Mayan weaving co-operatives, El Quetzal selected groups in San Antonio Palopó and San Juan La Laguna, both on Lake Atitlan and also purchases products from the Ruth Y Nohemi co-op in Chichicastenango and various family-owned businesses in Panajachel. In 2001, the organization employed a young indigenous woman as its Guatemalan agent, and in 2002, the organization began funding women's literacy classes in the Palopó community.

El Quetzal's board meets monthly to work on business planning, product development and the literacy project. The organization purchases products from the co-ops, not on consignment, as part of its commitment. Current products include clothing, tote bags, purses, tableware, hammocks, hats and aprons. Each year several board members travel to Guatemala to refine current designs, talk about new products and maintain personal contact with the producers.

Linda Daniels, founder of El Quetzal, with students in the literacy class at San Antonio Palopó Co-op.

Emily's craft group, called Craft Night, is made up of twelve women who meet monthly at each other's homes, share a dinner and work on their own crafts. Several are quilters; Emily makes baskets; another does beading; some are fine artists; one generally works on her "real work" as an interior designer; and they all do sewing, embroidery, knitting, beading and other textile work. Last week, Emily had the whole group putting prices on El Quetzal products in preparation for sale at a Seattle folk music festival. All of the members of Craft Night help at El Quetzal sales and tamale dinner fundraisers and even make quilts to raffle off for the literacy project.

Next year, Emily plans to take the members of her craft group to Guatemala to meet the co-op women, take some weaving lessons and attend Semana Santa, the holy week leading up to Easter. Now there's a craft group getaway!

How you can help:
❶ Support fair trade work. Ask if vendors at fairs and retail outlets are members of the Fair Trade Association.
❷ Go to El Quetzal's Web site, www.elquetzal.org, read about the co-ops and purchase products.
❸ Make a donation to the organization to support the Palopó literacy project.
❹ Work with your craft group to sell El Quetzal's products to your friends before the holidays or at festivals and bazaars, or find outlets for them in your area.
❺ Start your own nonprofit organization to support indigenous artisans! You can contact the organization through the above Web site to find information about El Quetzal's model.

# Our favorite Web crafters

If ever there was a fountain of wonderful ideas for craft projects, the Web is it. Now there's never an excuse for being fresh out of ideas, with hundreds just a click away. Many sites are a bit dull, calling for predictable materials and creations, but if you poke around for a while, you'll uncover some real gems created by one or more crafty divas sharing a lighthearted sense of humor and truly inspired, fun projects. Here are some of our crafting heroes, blazing a path from the Internet straight to your craft table. And be sure to look at the links they provide for more crafty destinations.

## Crafty Chica

www.craftychica.homestead.com

Who is this crafty chica? "She is kitschy, thrifty & quirky. She takes naughty pleasure in slapping fresh paint on raw wood. She doesn't need to spend a lot of cash to make ultra hip artsy projects. She loves the smell of Magic Markers, especially the fruit-flavored ones." She's Kathy Cano-Murillo, known to thousands of lucky readers of *The Arizona Republic*, where she publishes a regular column. You can keep up with her creations on her wonderful Web site, bursting with enthusiasm (after all, this is a woman who owns eight glue guns, and they're all high-temp). Make a wind chime from a coffee mug, a purse out of placemats or patio lights with ping-pong balls. As Kathy's motto states, "Viva la D.I.Y!" (See interview with Kathy on page 23.)

## Not Martha

www.megan.scatterbrain.org/notmartha

This is one crafty young woman's blog, with projects under headings like Home Spa-erific, Faux Food, Temporary Home Improvement, and Stuff to Wear, which includes our favorite entry, "My third knitted thing! a complete failure!" Not Martha indeed! (See interview on next page.)

## Bea's Diary

www.beasdiary.com

Go to her archives, and then "Things to Make." Wouldn't you look great in a Brownie belt? Don't forget to add the glue gun holster.

## Crafty Gal

www.craftygal.com

You can sign up here to receive a fun newsletter from "a bunch of craft-happy folks working to inspire other creative types with projects, recipes, personal essays and interviews with those who craft for a living." Or search the archives; the "table" section is where the crafts happen, naturally.

## Get Crafty

www.getcrafty.com

This site answers a creative person's gnarliest questions, such as: How do I knit a bikini? How do I bake like a Buddhist? How do I turn a record into a flower pot? And how do I paint racing stripes on my car?

## Cate's Garage Sale Finds

www.catesgarage.com

Her section on "evil, evil crafts" is both hilarious and a cautionary tale to us all.

## She Made This

www.shemadethis.com

This site is billed as "a resource for grrls who create" and is a forum of ideas submitted by those aforementioned grrls.

And for artistic inspiration …

## Another Girl at Play

www.another.girlatplay.com

Summarized as "Women artists sharing their stories," this site doesn't provide specific project ideas but does offer inspiration for anyone wanting to make the big leap from an everyday, salaried existence into a financially dicey but highly rewarding creative field. Features of the site: profiles, a discussion list, a newsletter and a resources section.

## 20 Things

www.20things.org

Here's a site that organizes art swaps. Twenty people make twenty pieces of art and send them to each other during a period of twenty days. The results are posted on the site, where there are links to other fun collaborative art projects, such as …

**The 1,000 Journal Project**
www.1000journals.com
"One thousand blank journals are traveling from hand to hand throughout the world. Those who find them will add stories and drawings and then pass them along. This is an experiment, and you are part of it." What a great idea. And for more collaborative inspiration …

**The Art Doll Chronicles**
www.stampington.com/html/the_art_doll_chronicles.html
From Lesley Jacobs, a participant: "The idea was that each artist would make a doll and everyone would contribute to that doll, in the spirit of the doll, as it came through. As the dolls traveled they developed personalities ... and each was very different. It was challenging to respond to each artist's creation and try to add to it in a thoughtful and creative way. Everyone was stunned at the directions their dolls took while on their travels, and we were all delighted by the results. I know for a fact that none of us could have or would have taken some of the creative paths that others took for us. It was an amazing learning experience."

**Church of Craft**
www.churchofcraft.org
If you live in or plan to visit San Francisco, New York, Los Angeles, Seattle, Montreal or Stockholm, drop in for a worship session. Here's the mission: "The Church of Craft aims to create an environment where any and all acts of making have value to our humanness. When we find moments of creation in our everyday activities, we also find simple satisfaction. The power of creating gives us the confidence to live our lives with all the love we can. By promoting creativity, we offer access to a nondenominational spiritual practice that is self-determined and proactive."

MEGAN REARDON

## Our questions for Not Martha

**❶ Why do you think there is such a surge of interest in people learning to do things with their hands?**
I have no idea. I can answer for myself, however: It was a reaction to my first job. I wrote code and Java script for Web sites, which involved sitting in a sterile cubicle in front of a flickering computer screen all day long. I found myself searching for small projects to fulfill a creative impulse, and making lip balm was my first one.

**❷ What is your favorite adhesive and why?**
I'm going to have to go with clear silicon sealer for making marble magnets. It is deliciously gooey.

**❸ How did "Not Martha" get started, and what are your dreams for the site?**

I needed to store my recipe for lip balm in a place where I could find it again and easily share it with friends. At the same time I had been bringing small things into work and people would remark, "You're such a Martha," and I would think, "No I'm not." I was surprised and pleased with the response to the site. I get great feedback and ideas from all over the world and a lot of answers when I get things completely wrong. It's like a conversation every day.

**❹ Have you experienced something powerful happening when women get together around making crafts? Do you think the same could be applied to men?**
Oh, sure, having a constructive focus which allows for conversation relaxes everyone. Also, it is a great way to meet and get to know people you otherwise would not. I don't see why the same couldn't apply to men. When I look at traditionally masculine pastimes like car repair or fishing, it seems like the same thing to me.

CHRIS VIOLA

KATHY CANO MURILLO

## Our questions for the Crafty Chica

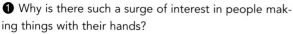

❶ Why is there such a surge of interest in people making things with their hands?

People want individual style; they want to wear or display things to make other people go, "Oooo, where did you get that?" It feels so good to say, "Oh, it's just a little something I whipped together." There are so many mass-produced items out there, the only way to truly achieve an individual style is to make your own custom designs. It's also a matter of money. Many people can't afford, say, a set of marble magnets for twenty dollars. So, automatically the wheels start turning and they figure out how to make their own for a fraction of the cost. According to the Hobby Industry Association, crafting is a twenty-six billion dollar a year business. There are vast resources to find help in making things from books to magazines to Web sites. Directions for making just about anything can be found readily, it seems.

❷ Who are some of your craft heroes?

My ultimate craft inspiration is my grade school art teacher (grades two through seven). She never gave me good grades in art class, never chose to hang my completed projects on the wall in the cafeteria. It was devastating at that age! I vowed for the rest of my life to prove her wrong about my artistic ability. Funny how those things stick with us! My real crafty heroes are women who have turned their personalities and passions into hands-on professions.

❸ What is your favorite adhesive and why?

I have three and I use them for different purposes in this order: E6000 Industrial Strength Craft Glue (still to this day, I have yet to find something it doesn't hold), Elmer's white glue (yes, old-school style! I use it on everything from decoupage to papier mâché and buy it by the gallon), and hot glue (I use a dab of it to hold something in place while the E6000 is curing).

❹ What's your favorite craft material?

Glitter is my crafty strong point and, at times, my weakness. I've been addicted to the shiny stuff since grade school, which is maybe why I freaked out my art teacher. In my studio I have every kind and color imaginable—squeezeable, squirtable, dry micro, brush-on, shake-on, etc. Outside my studio I have glitter pens, glitter paper, glitter nail polish—sheesh, glitter over-load. I love that glitter represents unity and strength in numbers—one fleck is barely visible, but a pile of it is stunning! There isn't a day when I don't have a glitter fleck on my face or in my hair.

❺ Have you experienced something powerful happening when women get together around making crafts?

Women are great at trying new ideas and sharing tips and techniques. Plus, when they get together to make things, that's when you get some of the best life stories. I once taught a workshop with twelve women, and we covered childbirth, depression, marriage and weird things that got stuck in our hair at one time or another. It becomes a community adventure, not just a "make and take" kind of session. I come from a family of crafters, and we have a blast getting together to make things for parties and weddings.

❻ Do you ever craft with men?

I paint every day with my husband in our studio and it has made our relationship stronger. We love to watch movies together while we work. But, as a whole, I don't think men have the same outlook. Theirs is more related to getting together to fix a friend's car or help each other out. They get it done and go. Even my hubby won't use the word "craft"; he likes "working on art stuff" instead.

# The right adhesive for the job

If you are as dilletante-ish as we are about crafts—that is, you have no time to become an expert on anything, flitting from one project to the next—you may appreciate this run-down that simplifies the array of adhesive choices we have today. Then again, you can skip this and go directly to a wonderful Web site, www.thistothat.com, that will tell you how to glue almost anything (this) to almost anything else (that), and also provides toxicity ratings. The site is produced by a Canadian theater prop builder with a sense of humor. Why does it exist? "Because," the site's tagline states, "people have a need to glue things to other things." Right-o.

Adhesives can be grouped into three categories. Within each there are dozens of products to choose from, most with overlapping applications. Ask around or find your own favorite brands.

✔ **Water-based adhesives.** Typically nontoxic with a nice aroma, like kindergarten. They often dry clear, but not as fast as those in the next category. Use with porous surfaces: paper, fabric, felt, ribbon, natural materials.

White glue, a.k.a. PVAs; tacky glue (bonds quicker than white glue and is flexible when dry); clear multi-purpose craft glue or gel (usually found with school supplies); glue sticks; library paste (for mounting papers with no wrinkling); wood glue; and water-based fabric glue.

✔ **Solvent-based adhesives.** These are not water-soluble and thus don't clean up with soap and water. They dry quickly and form strong bonds but may be flammable or toxic and require ventilation in use. Use with nonporous and semiporous surfaces.

Spray adhesive (for mounting images on backing); super glue; epoxy; all-purpose clear cement (not as strong as epoxy but less messy); silicone (an adhesive and sealant); high-tech adhesives (e.g., Crafter's Goop or E6000, crafters' favorites for strength and adaptability for many kinds of projects).

✔ **Hot-melt glues.** For easy and quick glue jobs or glue-intensive projects for which a durable bond is not essential.

Our favorite crafting accessory, the glue gun; the glue pot and microwaveable glue.

Here are the adhesives we couldn't live without. As you'll see, we tend toward the nontoxic options.

• **Tacky Glue.** Aleene's makes a quick-dry version. Some prefer Weldbond, a sort of super-PVA, because it works with some nonporous surfaces and thus is close to being multi-purpose.

• **YES! Paste.** A library paste for bookmaking and gluing papers with no wrinkling. We also love Coccoina Colla Bianca; it's Italian and smells delicious.

• **Mod Podge.** A staple collage glue and sealant, available in matte and glossy finishes. It dries quickly and works well with multiple layers. Caution: It will ripple paper.

• **Doublestick acid-free mounting tape.** For photos and more.

• **Glue sticks.** Permanent, removable or acid-free … just right for those ephemeral cut-and-paste projects.

• **Glue dots.** Sticky adhesive mini-blobs that adhere to almost anything. These don't form much of a bond but are great for kids' projects, rubber stamping and decorative work. No mess, no heat and they come in a nifty dispenser.

• **And of course, hot glue.** Don't bother with a mini gun. Get a mid-size or larger gun to keep that glue flowing. High-temperature guns are best for nonporous surfaces, larger areas and slower cooling times; low-temperature guns are better for delicate materials and are less likely to burn your fingers. We love the cordless models that recharge on a base, making you truly "wild with a glue gun."

# The art of scrounging

RULE NUMBER ONE: Always keep your eyes wide open for potential craft materials.

RULE NUMBER TWO: Never be afraid to ask.

Possessing these two skills in abundance will result in a full basement, attic, art room or closet of one-of-a-kind art supplies, not to mention membership in a not-too-exclusive club of "scrounge artists."

Recently we interviewed two of the world's finest *artistes de scrounge*, Cynthia and Charlotte (both members of Women Who Do Things with Their Hands), and asked them to share their scrounging secrets. They divulged (almost) all of their sources:

✔ **Phone books.** Look up a source for whatever item you are seeking. Ask for any surplus, remnants or damaged goods to donate for worthy art projects. Many will be glad to oblige.

✔ **Dumpsters.** Check out the dumpsters behind your favorite stores. Cynthia has a few favorite fabric stores where she has found whole bolts of fabric.

✔ **Sign companies.** Manufacturers of banners are your source for vinyl and rip-stop nylon leftovers. You also can request scraps of adhesive vinyl with peel-off backing for a range of crafting applications.

✔ **Film processors.** Ask for empty canisters that can be used for storing materials or assemblage pieces.

✔ **Large industrial surplus stores.** These outlets provide inspiration for using all types of "found" materials. In Seattle, for example, Boeing has a surplus store where you can purchase anything from roller bearings to pyramid-shaped rocks (used to tumble the rough edges off engine parts) to a row of airplane seats. The City of Seattle maintains a surplus store where ancient office supplies (huge ledger books, odd binding systems, weird Rolodexes) go for a song. Schools get rid of old chalkboards here. And when a library branch is renovated, old card catalogs appear; these are the best possible organizers of crafting tools and supplies.

✔ **Frame stores.** Ask friendly folks at a framing store to save scraps of mat board for you.

✔ **Thrift stores.** Look for bags of vintage buttons, bags of yarn and embroidery remnants, one-of-a-kind glass plates and glasses, Boy Scout and army medals, old books, back issues of *National Geographic*, games with lots of pieces, such as Scrabble, and "grab bags" in the toy section with parts of dolls, small trinkets and other riches for assemblage pieces.

✔ **Garage and estate sales.** This needs no explanation. You never know what you'll find here.

✔ **The dump.** Many small-town disposal centers have a give-away section where you can find the most amazing things: old record albums (some of the covers are suitable for framing!), bicycle parts, wash tubs, old photo albums … yep, you name it.

Sharing a love for scrounging truly cements a friendship. Only another scrounger will happily pitch in and help a fellow craftista move to a new home, knowing full well the amount of trips it will take to empty that garage or basement and get it set up again in a new location. Only a fellow craftnik will share your delight at finding a lovely purple plunger at the dump. Our groups include those with clutter-free homes and those with wall-to-wall adornment, but all make room somewhere for a stash of trashy treasure.

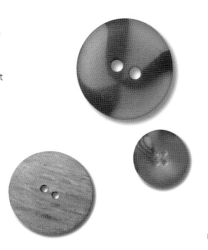

# Fun at the copy shop

For years, I have been a late-night visitor to my local copy center. I have seen managers and employees come and go, new machines introduced and the floor layout altered. I feel fairly certain I could step in at a moment's notice and work a staff member's shift if necessary. Why this fascination with photocopy machines? It's because I have found countless ways to use small reproductions of photos in a variety of craft projects, from portable shrines (page 120) to matchbox homages (page 124 ) to handmade books (page 78). Manipulating images for these projects has turned me into a self-serve color-copying zealot. Here are a few tips for zealots-in-the-making. Granted, all machines are not alike, but I have found these simple guidelines to be applicable to most. Of course, you can do all of this at home with a scanner, a computer, photo software and a color printer. But making copies can be simpler and more social.

—Christine

## Make multiple images at a reduced size!!

❶ Compute your reduction. If you know the dimensions you want to reduce to, borrow a proportion wheel to do a quick conversion from the dimensions of your original. Remember that reductions shrink the length and the width separately. So a 50 percent reduction will cut the length in half and the width in half, resulting in an image a quarter of the size of your original. Thus, if I want to reduce a 4" x 6" (10cm x 15cm) photo to fit on the lid of a matchbox, I reduce somewhere between 25 and 33 percent. Enter your reduction percentage using the pre-set options or the VARIABLE settings.

❷ Find the OUTPUT format on the machine. Generally this will offer a REPEAT IMAGE option. You have two choices under this category: AUTOMATIC, which gives you the maximum number of images that will fit on a sheet of paper, or VARIABLE, which enables you to set the number of repeats. When you choose the latter, it will ask you to indicate the number of rows and columns. I generally ask for two rows and three columns to allow a white border around each image.

❸ To change the color of a black-and-white print, look for COLOR OUTPUT and choose a color. There will be a place on the top of the printer where you can use a wand to choose a color from a palette of different hues. Choose a light brown for a sepia effect.

## Make a personalized journal!!

❶ Purchase or scrounge pieces of colored mat board for the cover. Cut to your desired size.

❷ For the pages, purchase medium-weight cardstock (markers and watercolors won't bleed through) and trim with a paper cutter to fit your cover. Make the height the same as your cover height and the width ¼" (6mm) smaller.

❸ Select a coil bind at the copy shop and hand over the pieces for assembly. Be sure to specify that you want coil, not comb, binding. This usually costs about four dollars.

❹ Cut a small window in the front cover and mount one of your photo reductions inside it. Presto! A beautiful journal.

## More fun at the copy center!!

• Transfer images to cloth, as for the pillow project on page 46.
• Create the pages for a handmade book, and before assembling it, make several sets of reductions. For example, a 4" x 6" (10cm x 15cm) book reduced by 55 percent with the automatic repeat image will make three copies per page. Then, cut and paste the pages into tiny books to give to kids, friends or family members.
• Make reduced copies of photos for handheld games, such as the ones on pages 94–95, or for sticking faces into printed pictures to create funny new images.

# Gift ideas for anyone with the craft chromosome

Important events in our lives deserve recognition. It's nice to receive a lovely handcrafted gift for a big birthday, the happy conclusion of a job search, perhaps even the happy conclusion of a marriage … and it's also awfully nice to be the recipient of materials and tools (and even time) for making things yourself. Here's a list arranged in order from small stocking stuffers all the way up to our to-die-for items for inspired giving among craft-group friends and to give suggestions to those who give to you.

• OUR NUMBER-ONE GIFT: a custom-decorated art box, completely stocked (see pages 28 and 29).

### $
• bag of buttons
• small magnet rounds
• bottles of glitter
• bone folder
• blank books for ideas and sketches
• customized collection of adhesives
• glass cutter
• extension cords
• set of clamps
• selection of fancy papers
• long-arm stapler

### $$
• cordless glue gun
• T-square ruler
• self-healing cutting mat
• ergonomic stapler
• ergonomic scissors
• craft knife set
• set of linoleum cutters and linoleum blocks
• tin snips
• tile snips
• assortment of jewelry pliers
• wire cutters
• cordless drill
• all-in-one tool set
• Japanese-style saw
• palm sander
• blender (used for crafts)
• iron (same as above)
• paper cutter
• rivet gun and rivets
• magnifier lamp
• Full-spectrum light on stand [Ott-Lite (fluorescent) or Chromalux (incandescent)]
• books full of visuals—colors, textures, designs, folk art, international culture
• gift certificate from favorite art supply or craft store, catalog or Web site

### $$$+
• craft retreat—provide a baby sitter, excuses for the boss, a place to go and whatever else is necessary to help someone get away and recharge her creative batteries
• sewing machine
• potter's wheel and small kiln
• flat file for papers
• drafting table
• workbench
• mobile air cleaner
• space for crafting (a closet, a corner of a room, an entire room, even a studio!)
• cabinet with craft trays (e.g., Debcor tray cabinet, made of steel and on casters)
• your very own color copy machine (only about $25,000 for a decent one)
• getaway cabin for weekend crafting extravaganzas (as long as we're thinking big)

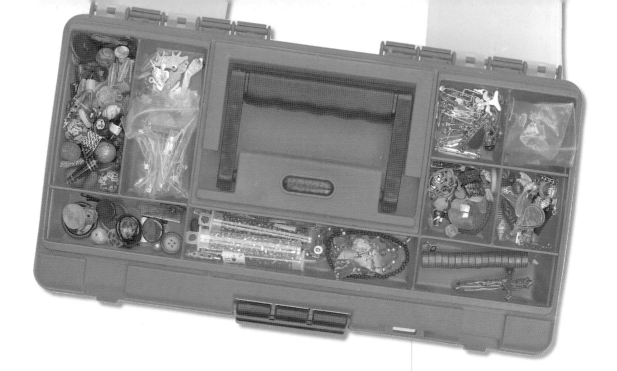

# Anatomy of a portable art box

I used to carry my supplies around in a beat-up old lime green fishing tackle box. Eventually the handle broke and I had to move on. My family created a new box, custom painted, and presented it to me on Mother's Day. Now I feel like a real professional—like Dr. Craft making house calls. In fact, this box is always in my car, ready to go. Create one for yourself, and don't leave home without it.

—Christine

**LID TRAY**
- small round magnets
- prized buttons
- single earrings
- pin and earring makings
- milagros and charms
- special beads
- crucifix pocketknife

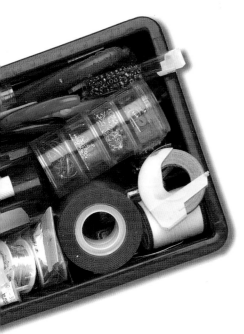

## MIDDLE LEVEL

- tweezers
- scissors
- pliers (three sizes)
- ruler
- glass cutter
- wire cutter
- tubes of seed beads
- fabric paint
- super glue
- glue stick
- book tape
- three different gauges of wire
- jewelry supplies (eye pins, chain links, fasteners)
- sample matchbox projects
- glitter pens
- homeopathic remedy for eye strain
- needle and thread
- hole punch

## BOTTOM BIN

- copper foil tape
- bag of sequins
- bottles of glitter
- small pieces of uncut glass
- favorite images reduced on a photocopier to a variety of sizes
- scraps of wrapping paper
- bag of shells
- bag of small figures
- bottles of acrylic paint
- glues
- box o' beads
- gold-sprayed Altoid boxes
- gold foil
- watercolors
- pens
- measuring tape
- glue gun!

BEADS & BAUBLES

# Lucky charm bracelet

Children are fascinated by their grandmothers' charm bracelets, packed with precious little souvenirs of travels through Europe and lockets with tiny photos inside. Why wait until you're a grandmother? Gather all those lucky charms out of the bottoms of desk drawers and dishes on your bureau, and put them around your wrist where they can give you good luck wherever you go. This is a project that will make you feel like a jewelry maker, even if you've always found jewelry-making intimidating.

—Kitty

### WHAT YOU'LL NEED
- jewelry chain, one or two strands, to fit
- nylon-coated bead stringing wire
- super glue with fine drop applicator
- string-through bead tips
- charms
- rounded needle-nose pliers
- jump rings
- clasp

## Making your bracelet

✔ Some things are easy to attach to a charm bracelet, such as charms designed for this purpose; just attach a jump ring and attach that to the chain. Other "charms" aren't as easy. If there's a hole through a charm, such as the old New York subway token on a bracelet below, string it on a piece of wire and attach it to a bead tip, which you then attach to the chain. The most difficult charms are those without a hole. You'll have to tie and glue wire around these, and then use a bead tip to attach them to the bracelet.

✔ Here's how a bead-tip works: ❶ String wire around or through your object, ❷ tie an overhand knot to bring the two wire ends together, ❸ string these up through the bottom of a bead tip, ❹ tie another overhand knot in the wire, ❺ situate the knot inside the bead-tip bowl, ❻ dab a tiny drop of super glue on the knot, ❼ use the needle-nose pliers to clamp the two halves of the bead tip together, ❽ clip off the excess wire and ❾ attach the loop of the bead tip to the chain. Use a rolling motion with the needle-nose pliers to close the loop of the bead tip.

✔ Attach the clasp ends to the ends of the chain(s).

✔ VARIATION: Use strands of beads with charms hung intermittently as the basis of your bracelet.

✔ TIP: There's a product from the folks at Shrinky Dinks that enables you to use an inkjet printer to transfer graphics, photos and other images onto plastic sheets and then shrink them down into little charms. Way cool! To order, go to www.shrinkydinks.com.

### Ambition Scale

# Sunglasses leash

Some years ago I returned from Johannesburg with a bunch of these colorful tethers as gifts for friends, who wore them to exhaustion. With no trips to South Africa planned for the near future, we had to re-create them, this time using strong wire for stringing the beads to give them greater longevity.

—Kitty

## Making your leash

✔ Measure and cut a 52" (132cm) piece of wire. Find the midpoint and bend it so you have two parallel strands.

✔ String beads onto 1½" (4cm) of wire so equal numbers of beads straddle the midpoint. String one end of an eyeglass loop over the beads. This will be the loop at one end of your leash.

✔ String a row of beads (three, five or more depending on the size) over both wires together.

✔ Separate the wires again, and string a row of beads onto 1" (3 cm) or more of each of the wires, side by side. Then string another set of beads onto both wires together.

✔ Continue this pattern (wires side by side, then wires together), ending with one row of beads strung on the wires together with approximately 2" (5cm) of wire remaining. Tie a square knot in the wires and pull tight.

✔ Take one of the remaining strands of wire and string 1" (3cm) with beads. String an eyeglass loop over the beads. Tie the two tail ends of wire together with another tight square knot at the same point as the first knot. Tuck the ends of wire back through either side of the loop to hide them, and clip off any excess.

## Ambition Scale

5

# Button bracelet

These bracelets are a wonderful showcase for buttons that have special memories, such as ones from your grandma's coat or a child's favorite dress. Once you have started a collection of buttons, sort them by color and size. Jars full of buttons on a window sill are a cheerful reminder of your endless potential for creativity.

—Charlotte and Lynn

**WHAT YOU'LL NEED**
- buttons
- elastic
- heavy-duty thread to match elastic color
- needle

## Ready, set...

• Always be on the lookout for old buttons. Grandmothers, yard sales and estate sales are good sources. Occasionally, you can find bags of them at thrift stores. Fabric and craft stores often have tubs of buttons and sometimes offer sale prices when you purchase by the pound.

• Choose the color and width of elastic banding that best suits the bracelet you want to create. The elastic should be at least 1" (3cm) wide; we like to use a 1¼" (4cm) band to accommodate bigger buttons. If you want a really wide bracelet, sew two bands together. Elastic typically comes in black, tan and white; occasionally you can even find velvet elastic—very swanky. Make sure the elastic is tightly woven; the kind made for lingerie is too loose for a bracelet. If you can find it in rolls by the yard, tug on the different types until you find the elastic with the most stiffness and resistance.

## Making your bracelet

✔ Measure a piece of elastic the exact circumference of your wrist, then add 1" (3cm) to provide a ½" (1cm) on either end for finishing off.

✔ Decide whether you want a monochromatic or multicolored bracelet. Lay out your buttons in a pattern that you like, with smaller buttons behind bigger ones to create a layered look. Always have a few extra buttons on hand in case you need to adjust the pattern as you sew.

✔ Start sewing buttons onto the elastic, leaving a ½" (1cm) space at either end. Sew the buttons as closely together as possible so that the elastic band doesn't show when the bracelet is curved around your wrist. When you've covered the elastic, create a finished look by folding in the raw edges on either end and sewing them together. You can continue to add small buttons to accent your design once you have sewed your bracelet together, but it's much easier to sew most of the buttons on when the elastic is still flat.

Ambition Scale

# Refrigerator magnets

Is there any object in the world that cannot be adapted to become a refrigerator magnet? OK ... we mean any object smaller than a breadbox? Our groups have expanded on the concept of refrigerator art with many magnetized creations; explore these and then add your own. This project is about as easy as they come, perfect for destressing after a full day.

—Christine and Kitty

## Ready, set...

• Take a deep breath and assemble your materials. If that proves taxing, spend some time with your Serenity Garden (see page 122) and then return. Seriously, this is probably the easiest project in this book, so have fun!

• TIP: There's a new magnet on the scene! New to us, anyway. Neodymium iron boron (NIB) magnets—commonly referred to as just "neodymium" or "rare earth" magnets—are more powerful and cheaper than the previous king of the magnet world, samarium cobalt. How strong are they? Suffice it to say that pretty much anything you want to hang on your refrigerator, short of the kitchen sink, can be supported by a small rare earth magnet.

**WHAT YOU'LL NEED**
• any small glue-able objects: buttons, dominoes, Scrabble letters, keys from old typewriters, glass-topped gemstone cases (from jewelry supply stores), dice, foreign coins left in your pocket after a vacation ...
• small, round magnets available at craft stores
• glue gun

## Making your magnets

✔ Decide on the object that is to become a magnet in its new life and affix it to a magnet with a dab of hot glue. Experiment with layering and different materials, if so motivated, or leave each item solo in all its simple glory.

✔ VARIATIONS: Lisa layers three or four buttons, slightly off center, with thread sewn through the holes of the top button for That Special Touch. Jane spells friends' names out of Scrabble letters (the old wooden tiles, purchased at thrift stores) and mounts them on metal mesh to give as gifts. The mesh, also called "builder's fabric," can be purchased by the foot at hardware stores.

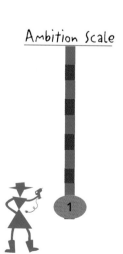

Ambition Scale

# Bead people

Bead people are great for key chains or for hanging on your rear-view mirror where they do a little dance as you drive along. My daughter taught me this project a number of years ago after learning it at a beading class. I introduced it to my group on a getaway weekend, and we discovered that it went very well with chocolate dessert. We were amazed by the varieties of "personalities" that emerged using the same techniques and materials and when fueled by chocolate.

—Christine

## Ready, set...

• You will need an assortment of beads, including tube-shaped ones for arms and legs, a larger one for the body, seed beads for the joints and a wide bead for the face. You can create this with polymer clay if you prefer.

### Ambition Scale

4

### WHAT YOU'LL NEED
- beads
- glittery yarn and thread for the hair
- thin-gauge wire for stringing
- felt or fabric for skirt (optional)
- needle-nosed pliers

## Making your bead person

✔ Cut two pieces of wire, one about 12" (30cm) long and the other about 24" (61cm). Fold each in half and twist them together at their centers. You will have four strands at this point, two short and two longer.

✔ Wrap strands of yarn or thread at the intersection of the four wires and tie them off. Then thread the four wires down through your "head" bead and on through a throat adornment.

✔ Take the two short wires and pull them out to either side to serve as arms. String a tubular bead on each for the upper arm, then a seed bead for each elbow, then another tubular bead for the forearm, another seed bead for the wrist. Create the hands using one or more beads for each. Use the needle-nosed pliers to pull the ends of the arm wires back up through the last couple of beads and then snip off the ends.

✔ String your "body" bead onto the two remaining long strands.

✔ Separate the two strands and add beads to each for thighs, knees, calves, ankles and feet. Finish off by reinserting the wire back up the last couple of beads to secure them and hide the wire. Then snip off the remaining wire.

# Slide photo magnets

My sister came up with this favor for the guests at my wedding. Now, whenever I visit friends' houses, I get to see our photo on their refrigerators—which is OK since I looked young and childless then (no bags under the eyes).

—Lynn

## Ready, set...

• Recommended: deluxe glass slide mounts with thin sheets of glass between which you sandwich your image.

• Go to a copy shop and make color copies of your photographs reduced to fit into a 1½" x 1" (4cm x 3cm) window. If you copy a standard 4" x 6" (10cm x 15cm) photo, for example, you will reduce it to 25 percent of the original size.

• If you wish to include a special message visible through the back of the frame, print it by hand onto the metallic paper or use a computer and printer to do so. Set up the document so that it can be cut into squares of 1¾" x 1¾" (4cm x 4cm) with a 1" (3cm) square message area.

### Ambition Scale

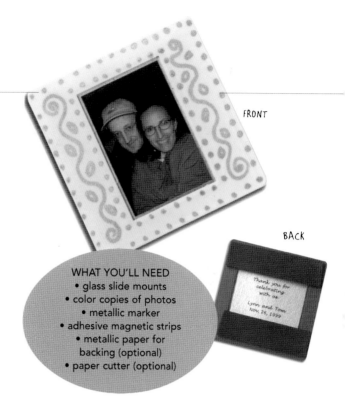

FRONT

BACK

**WHAT YOU'LL NEED**
• glass slide mounts
• color copies of photos
• metallic marker
• adhesive magnetic strips
• metallic paper for backing (optional)
• paper cutter (optional)

## Making your magnet

✔ Use scissors or a paper cutter to cut your photographs and the metallic paper into squares of 1¾" x 1¾" (4cm x 4cm).

✔ Pry apart a slide mount. Place a photo and a backing square together and then the message if you're including one. With the photo facing upward and the message downward, place them into the slide back and pop the white front on top. Snap into place. Your image should be perfectly framed inside the silver edging within the opening. If not, open and adjust.

✔ Use a metallic pen to decorate the plastic slide mount and allow to dry.

✔ Cut strips of magnet into 1½" (4cm) lengths. Peel off the adhesive backing and attach a strip to either side of the glass on the back of the slide mount.

# Bottle cap earrings

While living in West Africa, I was fascinated by the toys created by kids using all sorts of odds and ends—tires, tin cans and even discarded packaging from birth control pills! I began incorporating recycled materials in my own art, and bottle caps in particular became a source of inspiration. Any time I visit a new delicatessen, food co-op or grocery store, I stroll through the soda and beer section in search of new and different caps.

Better still are the rusty, bent and flattened caps I find just walking down the street. My friend Kay has joined in the bottle cap pursuit and plans to make a curtain out of the hundreds she has collected. It is a curious passion, but one that makes life a continual treasure hunt.

—Cynthia

## Ready, set...

• Notes on jewelry "findings": an earring wire is the wire loop that goes through a pierced ear, with a loop at the bottom for attaching decorative elements. A head pin is a bead wire with a flat end for attaching beads to the bottle cap.

Ambition Scale

6

## Making your earrings

✔ Make a marks for holes on the inside of your bottle caps. Make a mark at the top and one at the bottom of your earring, and then six additional marks equally spaced between them for a total of eight holes.

✔ Rest the bottle cap on a block of wood, position the nail at each marked spot, and tap with a tack hammer to punch holes.

✔ Cut the head pins to the desired length and string with beads to your liking. Insert the end of each beaded pin in a hole on the sides of the bottle cap, securing each wire end with a dot of hot glue onto the back of the bottle cap. Leave sufficient wire for bending the end over inside the cap.

✔ For the earring wire on top, thread one or two seed beads onto the wire, then insert it into the top hole, cut it to the appropriate length, and bend the end into a loop that allows the bottle cap to swing.

✔ For the dangle at the bottom of the earring, thread a charm and one or two beads on a head pin, insert into the bottom hole, cut the wire and bend into a loop around the edge of the bottle cap.

✔ Decorate the back to cover the messy wires. First, fill in the back of the bottle cap with hot glue, creating a level layer over the bead wire ends. Allow this to cool. Choose something to serve as the back surface of the earring—a small square of plastic with a button inside as shown at lower left, a piece of mirror, beads or glitter—and attach with hot glue.

**WHAT YOU'LL NEED**
- bottle caps
- large seed beads
- two earring wires
- head pins
- small block of wood for hammering
- materials for filling in back of earring: small plastic shapes, glitter, small pieces of mirror ...
- tack hammer
- glue gun
- felt tip pen
- charms
- long, thin nail

# Spiral bead bracelet

I love the notion that these bracelets are made on "memory wire"! How does one create a wire that can remember its shape and spring back into it no matter how many times it is contorted? Maybe the inventor of the Slinky toy created it. Without a doubt, it's the perfect wire for making a bracelet that easily coils around any number of wrist sizes.

Last summer I used this wire to create memory bracelets for my two partners in the Danskin Triathlon. I found small charms to commemorate the occasion and the unique personalities of my friends and strung them alongside tiny iridescent seed beads and other special beads. Cynthia and Charlotte use their formidable stockpile of beads from around the world to make one-of-a-kind spiral bracelets that are treasured as gifts by all of their friends. For those who are just venturing forth into jewelry making, this is a wonderful intro-ductory project.

—Christine

## Ambition Scale

2

## Ready, set...

• Decide on a theme for your bracelet. This can originate from a bead color and shape or an event like the one mentioned in the introduction. You can collect beads and charms on a trip to make a memory bracelet or create a birthday bracelet that showcases the unique personality and aesthetics of a friend.

## Making your spiral bracelet

✔ Cut the memory wire to the length you desire after wrapping it around your own wrist and determining the ideal number of coils. You can choose any number of coils from three to eight for someone with a really long arm. Allow extra length for bulky beads.

✔ Use needle-nose pliers to bend one end of the memory wire back against its natural coil to provide a "stop" for the beads. Then slip a small bead onto the opposite end of the wire to start the bracelet.

✔ Continue to add beads and charms, covering the length of wire. Finish by bending the end of the wire back against itself.

> **WHAT YOU'LL NEED**
> • memory wire (from jewelry supply or craft stores)
> • needle-nose pliers
> • an assortment of beads and charms (anything with a small opening for stringing)

# Photo pillow

This is a great gift for kids and adults, friends and relatives (or you can keep a pillow with a photo of a foe and use it as a punching bag). I have used many kinds of pillows from durable cotton to more elegant velvet in bright colors or more subtle ones depending on the image the pillow is meant to complement.

—Kitty

## Ready, set...

• For this project you can make your own pillow, of course, but it's so easy to purchase an inexpensive, ready-made throw pillow with fabric and trim colors to match a photo's colors and mood.

• To transfer a photo to cloth, you have three options. For me it is easiest to take a photo to a copy or photo shop that can transfer images onto cloth using a professional heat press. If there's no one nearby with this capability, you can purchase heat-transfer paper. Use a color photocopier to print the image onto the paper, then transfer the image from the paper onto the cloth using an iron. You can also use an inkjet printer to print a digital file onto special photo-transfer paper (generally available at craft and office supply stores or from quilting supply Web sites)

and then iron it on. If you want to explore this craft niche further, there are many good books for quilters that will tell you all you need to know.

• Depending on the size of your original photo, you may want to enlarge or reduce. If so, experiment on a copy machine first to determine the correct percentage. Be sure to supply the percentage you want when you drop off the photo and cloth at the copy center.

• Choose a decorative trim in keeping with the dimensions of your pillow and the image. You can use ribbon, bric-a-brac, strips of brocade with finished edges or a fancy trim sold by upholsterers. You will need enough to go around all four edges of your image, plus a little extra.

• Turn the edges of the cloth under and iron, leaving a small border of white around the edge of the image (slightly narrower than the width of your trim). The trim will cover the white border, and the turned hem will ensure that no frayed edges are visible beneath the trim.

## Making your pillow

✔ Sew the cloth image onto the center of the front side of the pillow, using a running stitch along the white border.

✔ Starting in one corner, sew the trim around the edge of the image. Using tiny basting stitches, secure it to the white border, making sure the border is hidden completely.

✔ When you come to the next two corners, fold the trim under and tack it down to create a mitered corner as you proceed to the next edge. When you've gone the whole way around, cut the end of the trim, leaving a small tail. Tuck this under and tack it down to achieve a finished border.

✔ Add tassels to the pillow corners if you feel so inspired.

**WHAT YOU'LL NEED**
- throw pillow
- piece of white 100% cotton broadcloth
- decorative trim
- sewing supplies
- photo
- heat-transfer or photo transfer paper (optional)

## Ambition Scale

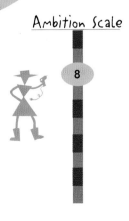

8

# Spirit dolls

## VARIATION I: WIRE

Two of our founding members, Sarah and Charlotte, started a tradition for "momentous life moments." They introduced a doll assemblage project from the Seattle Children's Museum, where they both worked. Some time later, when I was going into the hospital for surgery, our group made a doll to hang above my bed. When I woke up after surgery, she was the first thing I saw when I opened my eyes. This doll has been a steadfast companion ever since. I often send her out to keep watch over friends when they are going to the hospital for a procedure of one kind or another. She probably has been to every hospital in town.

Since then we have made dolls to commemorate birthdays, births, illnesses and passages in our lives. Each person can make a spirit doll individually, or the group can collaborate. With the latter, one individual begins the doll by forming a basic wire frame and then passes the frame to the next person, who starts to form the body with a strip of cloth. Around and around the group it goes, each embellishing and making the doll more glorious.

Consider this project for a girl's birthday or rite-of-passage party, a bridal shower or any other occasion with people who appreciate a ready supply of materials spread out on a table to be shared by all. Recently my group presented a workshop using this project at our local "Gilda's Club," a nationwide organization for people living with cancer. It was a very special evening as we watched members fashioning these dolls with intent and a sense of humor.

—Christine

## Making your wire spirit doll

✔ Create a simple frame out of wire or pipe cleaners: Fold a length of wire in half. Fold a round head from the middle, creased part. The rest of the wire will become the body and legs. Use additional wire to form the arms by twisting them around your starting wire. Your choice of wire and desired size of the doll will dictate your construction method. The goal here is to create the framework for your doll.

✔ From this point, be creative in building the body shape you desire. You can wrap strips of cloth around the frame to fill out the form or fold stuffing (cotton balls or cotton/polyester batting) over the wire frame to give the doll more shape before covering it with fabric.

✔ To make your doll even more special, give her a scented belly. Stuff a small muslin sack with potpourri or dried flowers (lavender buds and rose petals are both nicely aromatic), or fill it with uncooked rice that has been scented with your favorite essential oil. Or just use an

herbal tea bag that smells good. Attach this to the wire torso by wrapping strips of cloth around the sack and torso and then tucking in the cloth.

✔ If your doll cries out for facial features, use beads, embroidery thread, buttons or fabric paint to create just the right face. Or you may decide that your doll has just the right look without any additions.

✔ Add scraps of cloth, ribbon and yarn to make clothes and hair.

✔ Add beads, charms, dried flowers and any number of trinkets for the final adornments.

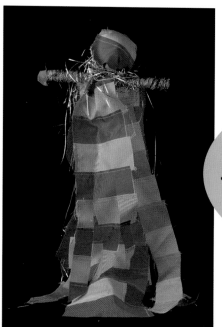

> **WHAT YOU'LL NEED**
> - pliable wire in various gauges
> - stuffing material (e.g., cotton balls, cotton/polyester batting)
> - soft scraps of fabric, felt, yarn, ribbon and trim
> - trinkets: charms, beads, old pieces of jewelry
> - miscellaneous adornments: buttons, feathers, pipe cleaners, sequins

## Ambition Scale

5

One summer, while listening to a reggae band at a music festival, I wandered over to a tent off to the side to see what was going on. It was mobbed with people—men and women, Rasta and artsy types, teens and grannies—making raffia spirit dolls.

My 3-year-old and I joined the fray, with everyone passing glue guns back and forth, digging through bins of beads, feathers and fabric, chattering about how inspired we were and dancing to the music at the same time. Since then I've found it a great activity not just for glue gunners' gatherings but also for special occasions, including a wedding shower where we made various "versions" of the bride-to-be and presented them all to her as a raffish spiritual dowry.

—Kitty

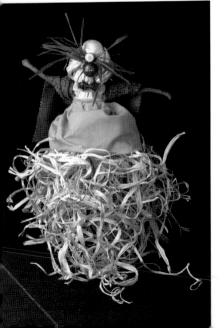

Ambition Scale

5

## Making your raffia spirit doll

✔ Grab a handful of raffia as if you were holding a horse's tail at its midpoint. You'll want a healthy amount, about enough to fill the circle you make with your thumb and index finger as you hold the shank. Now "comb" out the strands to make them more or less even and aligned.

✔ With both hands at the midpoint twist the shank as if you were wringing out a dishtowel. As you twist tightly, the raffia shank doubles over and around to create the doll's head. Hold the tight twist in one hand and use the other to wrap a pipe cleaner around it. Twist the pipe cleaner

WHAT YOU'LL NEED
• bags of dyed raffia
• sticks about the thickness of your pinkie finger
• wire or pipe cleaners
• fabric scraps
• adornments

tightly around the doll's neck to secure the head; wrap it around a second time and tie it off to make sure it will hold.

✔ Place a 12" (30cm) stick vertically inside the doll's "body" and push it up from below into her neck where the pipe cleaner will hold it in place. This stick is handy for holding your doll as you embellish her. Take another stick, 8" (20cm) long, and place it cross-wise through the raffia (on top of the vertical stick) just below the pipe cleaner. Take another pipe cleaner and tie it around the doll's torso to give her a bodice and waistline (though really it's to hold the stick in place). Now she has arms.

✔ Decorate as with the wire spirit doll, sparing no ornament. Trim off stray raffia strands as desired.

# Safe passage pouch

A few years ago my family went on a journey to Central and South America. The night before I left, my sisters presented me with a small pouch they had made. Inside were all sorts of talismans of good luck: angels, fairy dust, magical pebbles, charms and a wonderful note wishing me a grand adventure and safe passage. Needless to say, the pouch went everywhere I did, and in tough travel moments it buoyed my spirits to sort through the objects and think of my sisters back home.

In many cultures a pouch filled with shielding magic is a necessity for traveling on life's journeys. While living in South Africa, Kitty's friends there made her a pouch filled with "muti," an array of objects with protective powers, for her journey back to the U.S. Pouches like these would fit the bill for all kinds of passages: living away from home for the first time, getting married, getting unmarried, a first child. Who in your life needs a safe passage pouch?

—Christine

## Making your pouch

✔ Cut a rectangle of fabric. For a small pouch, cut a 5" x 3½" (13cm x 9cm) piece. Increase the dimensions proportionately for larger pouches.

✔ Iron a ¼" (6mm) triangular fold ❶ at both corners of one of the long edges of the fabric.

✔ Fold this same edge over ❷ and sew a ¼" (6mm) seam along the entire length.

✔ Fold again ❸ and sew a ½" (1cm) seam for the drawstring.

✔ Put right sides together and sew a seam from the bottom corner across the bottom edge and up the side to the opening. ❹ Stop sewing just below the drawstring channel.

✔ Turn right side out and use the large needle to pull a ribbon or cord through the channel for the drawstring.

✔ Embroider designs or add charms or beads to the outside of your pouch. Fill with treasures.

**WHAT YOU'LL NEED**
• sewing machine
• needle with large eye
• scraps of fabric for the pouch (velvety, shimmery fabrics lend a magical feel)
• embroidery thread or ribbon for the drawstring
• appropriate talismans

❶  ❷  ❸  ❹

Ambition Scale

④

# Dream pillow

This is not a functional object; it isn't meant to reduce eye puffiness during sleep or make you drowsy. Yet it is not merely decorative, either. This is an important accessory for your dream processing. When you place it under your pillow before going to sleep, it sucks bad-dream elements from your pillow and plants good-dream seeds in their place.

I made my first dream pillow in third grade when I was staying home sick all by myself for the first time. I gathered some fabric and stuffing and made a little heart-shaped pillow from remnants of Dacron polyester given to me by my Grandma Gladys. Over the years I have made dream pillows for friends and family members whenever I felt they needed one. Now I use fragrant stuffing for the added benefit of inducing floral-scented dreams.

—Sarah

## Ready, set...

• When collecting materials, choose favorite colors, textures and objects to use in your design.

• VARIATIONS: As filling for your pillow, you can use naturally scented materials such as dried lavender blossoms or rose petals, or use fiberfill or rice as stuffing and add a sachet soaked with drops of an essential oil for scent.

## Making your pillow

✔ Cut two pieces of fabric for your pillow. They can be any shape but keep them small enough to tuck under a standard-sized pillow. Leave a ½" (1cm) seam allowance.

✔ Embroider or decorate the fabric that will be the top of the pillow.

✔ Place the right sides of the two fabric pieces together, facing each other, and stitch along the seam line most of the way around the pillow, leaving a 2" (5cm) opening for stuffing.

✔ Turn right side out and fill with your choice of stuffing, sewing up the remaining opening by hand.

✔ Add small beads or other talismans to bring forth the best dreams possible.

Ambition Scale

4

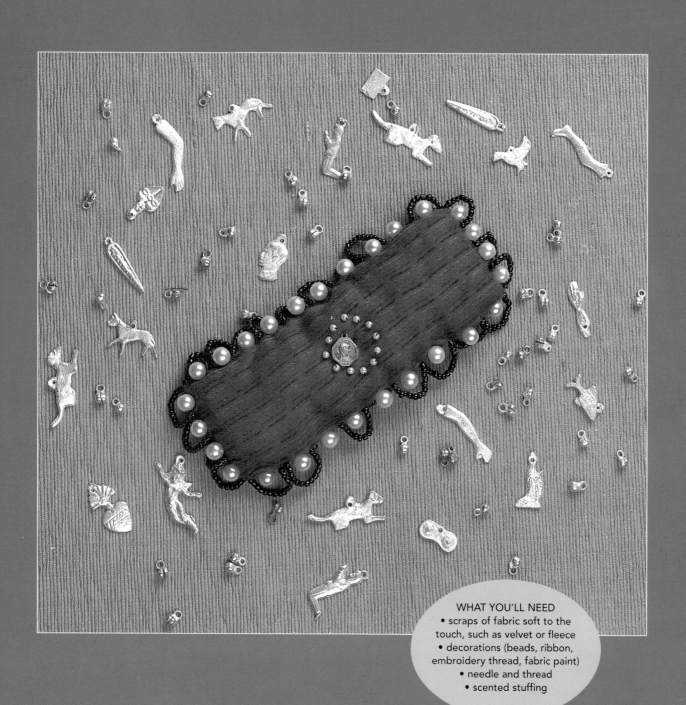

# Sleeping bag for dolls

A few years back I was at a neighborhood bazaar and saw a crowd of young folks around a booth. When I investigated I found that the objects of desire were sleeping bags for Beanie Babies! They were by far the biggest hit of the bazaar. I filed the idea away and later made a modified version for my daughter's favorite doll; henceforth Josefina was no longer cold on camping trips. You can create a bag for any doll or stuffed animal. Who knows—this project may even get Barbie dolls into the outdoors.

—Christine

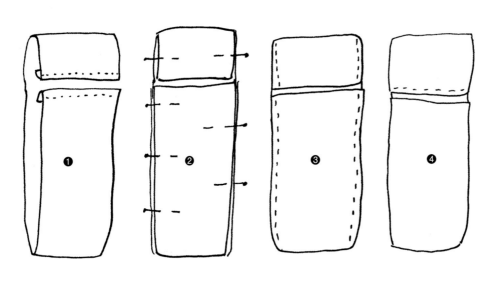

## Ready, set...

• Do not let a lack of sewing experience deter you from this project. You can sew by hand or on a machine, whichever is easiest for you. If you can sew a straight seam on the machine you're all set.

• Be ever-vigilant for polar fleece remnants at the fabric store. They can be used for myriad projects including this one.

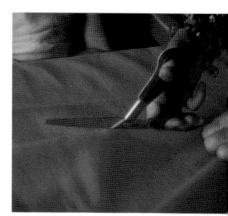

## Making your sleeping bag

✔ Measure the length and width of your intended sleeper for the bag. Multiply the length by 2½, and add 2" (5cm) to the width. For example, my doll is 10" (25 cm) long and 5" (13cm) wide. My piece of polar fleece will need to be 25" (64cm) long and 7" (18cm) wide. Cut a piece of polar fleece to these dimensions.

✔ At each of the short ends of your length of fabric, ❶ turn under the edge and stitch across.

✔ Put right sides together (your hems will be on the outside), and then pull approximately 5" (13cm) of one end of the length of fabric up for the pillow. The remaining length, folded in half, will form the sleeping bag. Fold the pillow portion in half, as well, and pin the sides of the pillow and the sides of the sleeping bag on each side. ❷ The hemmed edges of each should just touch one another.

✔ Sew a seam along the length of the pillow and bag on each side, ❸ leaving a ⅛" (3mm) seam allowance.

✔ Turn the bag and the pillow right side out. ❹ Put a small amount of stuffing into the pillow pocket and then sew it shut.

**WHAT YOU'LL NEED**
• scraps of polar fleece
• pillow stuffing
• embroidery thread
• sewing supplies

# Handwoven scarf

A trip to Paris can inspire all kinds of creativity. I was heading there on a trip and decided I needed a scarf of a certain length and color. Could I wait until I arrived and find the perfect scarf in Paris? Mais non! We Americans must make an effort to swathe our necks properly, especially on Parisian soil. I determined that it was necessary to create this ideal scarf myself and would not let the fact that I don't knit or weave stand in my way. Back in a foggy nook of my brain I recalled the cardboard looms I had made with my kids for simple weavings and then expanded on the idea. Nécessité truly does breed invention!

—Cynthia

## Ready, set...

• Visit a fabric store and ask for an empty cardboard bolt.

• Gather a selection of yarns that speak to you in color and texture. This is an opportunity to use up small amounts of yarn left over from knitting projects. If you are not a knitter, you might ask knitting friends to put aside remainders for you. You can also occasionally find bags of yarn remnants at thrift stores or knitting stores.

• To prepare your loom: Mark cutting lines at the top and bottom of the cardboard bolt, beginning 2" (5cm) in from each side and continuing at ¾" (2cm) intervals spaced equally across. For the example shown, I made sixteen notches across the top and bottom of the bolt; you can increase or decrease this amount but make sure it is an even number.

### Ambition Scale

5

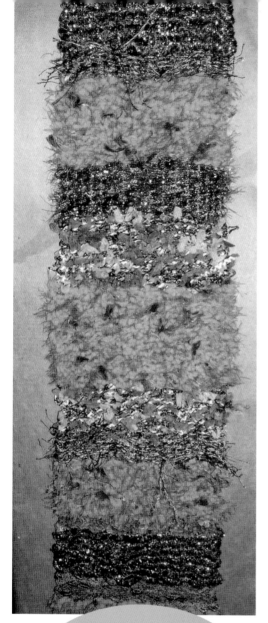

## Making your scarf

✔ Choose a "warp" or background color. Starting at one end of the bolt, attach the length of warp yarn into the first notch with about 4" (10cm) hanging loose. Loop the yarn up and into the corresponding notch at the other end and then over the back of the bolt into the next notch below. Continue looping up, over, down and around until you have wedged the yarn into all of the notches. Cut the yarn, again leaving a 4" (10cm) tail.

✔ Now you are ready to weave! Choose your first "weft" yarn and thread it into the needle. Begin weaving about 6" (15cm) from the top of the loom. Weave the needle over and under the warp yarns across the width of the loom, leaving a tail of about 4" (10cm) at the start point (you will weave this tail up along the edge of the scarf after you have woven a few inches). When you pull your needle out at the end of the first row, pull your yarn through gently.

✔ Start the next row by going over the last warp thread (if you just went under it) or under it (if you just went over it), and continue weaving. As you get to the end of each row, be sure not to pull the yarn too tightly or your scarf will not be of equal width.

✔ After you have woven three or four rows, use a wide-toothed comb to gently push the rows down, bringing them together for a tighter weave. This process will also help keep your rows neat.

✔ Change yarns according to your fancy. When you finish off a yarn at the end of a row, weave a tail of about 4" (10cm) in and out of the row immediately preceding it. Trim off the excess. Then begin a new color in the same way that you began weaving.

✔ Continue weaving until you reach a point 6" (15cm) from the bottom of the loom. Finish off your last yarn end. Cut through the warp threads at the very top and bottom of the loom. Tie off the ends by knotting pairs together—yarn #1 to yarn #2, yarn #3 to yarn #4, and so on. Now you're ready for Paris!

**WHAT YOU'LL NEED**
- an assortment of yarns of different lengths, textures, and colors—the thicker the better
- cardboard from an empty bolt of fabric
- long tapestry needle with an eye large enough for yarn
- wide-toothed comb

# Hot water bottle cover

I have seen covers for hot water bottles made of terry cloth—and monogrammed, no less—available in various catalogs. Scraps of leftover fleece fired some synapses in my brain (fleece, after all, being the penny-pincher's cashmere) and another craft project was born.

—Kitty

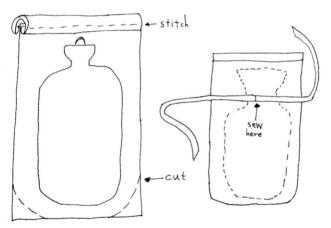

## Making your cover

✔ Measure your hot water bottle and add 3" (8cm) to the width and length (to allow for the water in the bottle and for the cinching of the neck). Double a piece of fleece and cut out two rectangular pieces of fleece at the same time to these dimensions. Using a pencil (for white fleece) or a piece of chalk (for colored fleece), lightly draw the rounded outline of the bottom corners of the bottle onto the fleece. Then cut along the lines to create the rounded edges.

✔ If you wish, sew a colored border to the top/square edge of the two pieces of fleece; just wrap a strip of fleece in a contrasting color at the top of each piece, tuck edges under, pin and stitch across. Or you can leave the top a raw edge; fleece won't fray.

Ambition Scale

5

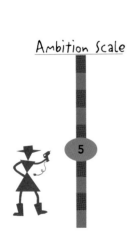

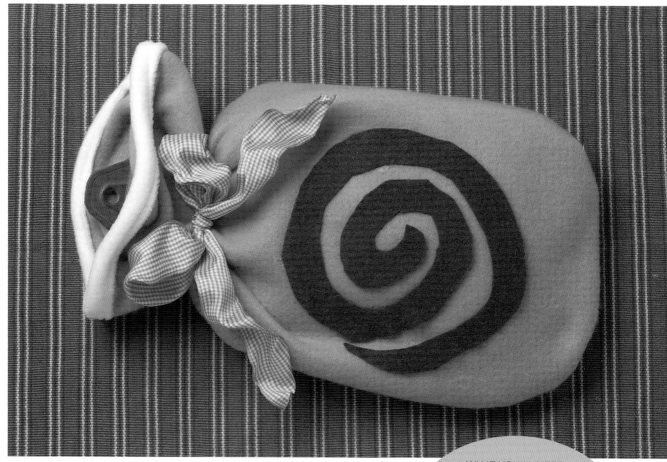

✔ With right sides together, run the side, bottom and other side through the sewing machine with a ½" (1cm) seam allowance. Turn right side out. You now have a pouch into which to insert the hot water bottle.

✔ Cut pieces of felt into a design and use fabric glue to apply them to the fleece. I like to use Beacon's Fabri-Tac permanent adhesive. Although it smells like something you don't want to spend a lot of time sniffing if you prize your brain cells, it grabs and dries quickly and is washable.

✔ Using needle and thread, attach a length of ribbon to the cover at the "neck" of the bottle, tacking it to the back side in the center. Turn over and tie the ribbon in a bow around the bottle neck to hold the cover in place.

**WHAT YOU'LL NEED**
- sewing machine
- hot water bottle
- pencil or chalk
- half a yard (46cm) of fleece
- 20-24" (50-60cm) length of ribbon
- thread to match fleece color(s)
- felt
- fabric glue
- needle and thread

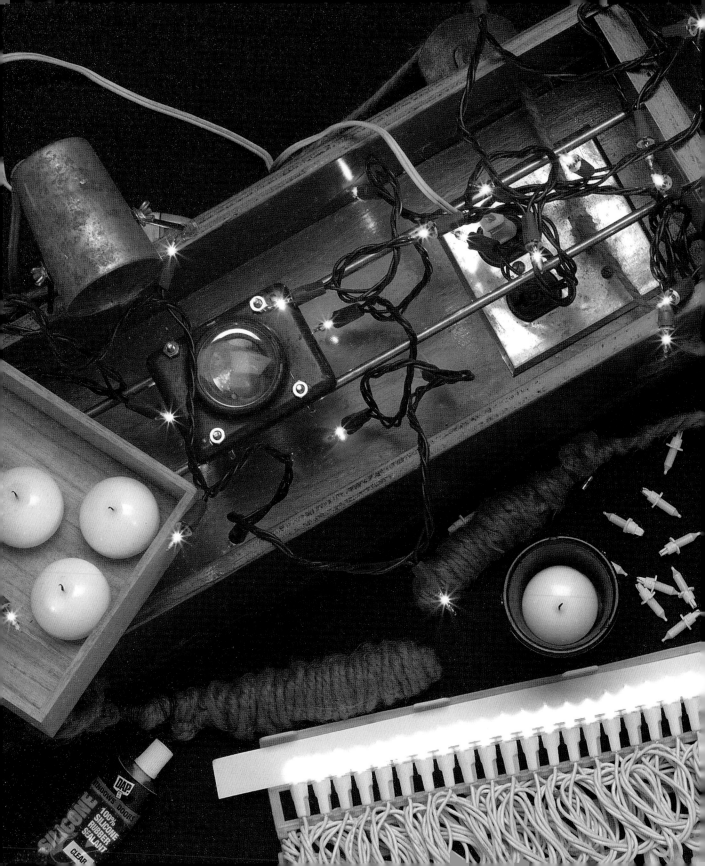

LIGHT

# scallop shell lights

Do you have some scallop shells gathering dust in a bowl because they look beautiful on the beach but lose their luster at home? Try illuminating them from the inside; lights make the shells glow and show the variation in shades. Friends liked mine so much that I ended up making a bunch for Christmas presents. A few years later, this project showed up in Martha Stewart's magazine. You know, I was sure I saw her peeking in my windows a while back ...

—Kitty

## Ready, set...

• Gather pairs of scallop shells, one pair for each bulb on your light string. I have used scallop shells from East Coast beaches—peachy, tawny and even zebra-striped—and shells from the pink, "singing" scallops available on the West Coast.

• Clean the shells thoroughly (you can throw them in the dishwasher without soap). When dry, rub the outsides with baby oil to bring out the color. The disadvantage to this natural treatment is that the oil will attract dust, but you can wipe them down and reoil them periodically. Or you can spray the shells with an acrylic spray—in gloss or matte finish, depending on your preference for shine.

**WHAT YOU'LL NEED**
• scallop shells
• decorator light string
• baby oil or acrylic spray
• glue gun or epoxy
• razor blade or craft knife

## Making your lights

✔ Fit two shells around each light with the wire going through the groove at the squared-off edges. Rub them together until you get a good fit. Lift up one shell and use a glue gun to spread lots of glue over and around the wire. Close the shell and hold until dry. If you find it hard to get a good seal with the glue gun method (perhaps because some baby oil has gotten inside the shell), try epoxy or E6000. This works well, but you must clamp the shells with rubber bands until they dry.

✔ On occasion, you will have to glue a shell more than once to get good adherence. The shells will never lie flat against each other as they did in nature, because the lighting cord protrudes on either side, but they will come together well enough to hold.

✔ At the end of the light string (the end without the plug, that is), separate the strands to form one loop that threads through the final pair of shells (see photo at right).

✔ Use a single edge razor blade or craft knife to trim off extra glue.

Ambition Scale

6

# Book lamp

This idea came to me in the basement of a Salvation Army store where I stood surrounded by bins of hardcovers selling for a quarter apiece. (That was a while ago; on a recent visit they were up to a dollar each. Now I would try to get books at the dump.) It was fun sorting through to find the nicest colors and the most compelling titles. At home I went through the books and kept the ones that looked like good reading, such as *Guiding Your Daughter to Confident Womanhood*, ca. 1964, and drilled a hole down the center of the rest. Some might consider it a sacrilege to do such a thing to a book, but there are many books in the world that would gladly find their way out of a musty bin and into your home, proudly shining in lamplight.

—Kitty

Ambition Scale

8

WHAT YOU'LL NEED
• hardcover books
• power drill and new drill bit
• lamp hardware
• razor knife

## Ready, set...

• The first step is a visit to your local lighting supply store, where you will ask a kind and knowledgeable person to help you assemble the hardware for your lamp. If you don't have such a store with such a person nearby, you can order from www.lampshop.com or www.nationalartcraft.com.

• For my lamp, the components are as follows (in ascending order): ❶ a nut and a washer, screwed onto ❷ a hollow, threaded rod that extends up through the books (invisibly) for 8" (20cm), and up to the light fixture (visibly) another 5" (13cm), ❸ the books, ❹ another washer that rests on top of the books, ❺ a brass sleeve that covers the visible portion of the threaded rod, ❻ the support (called a harp) for the shade, ❼ the light socket with power cord extending down through the hollow rod, ❽ a shade and ❾ a screw-on cap (called a finial) that holds the shade on the support. You also can choose among various styles and finishes for the decorative hardware to fit your vision.

• Note that the rod running through the books determines the height of your lamp. You can have the rod cut to any length to fit the number of books you are using and the height you want your lamp to be.

• Fair warning: It isn't easy to drill through a book. You should use the sharpest drill bit possible; it's worth purchasing a brand new one. I used a ¾" (2cm) bit to accommodate a

rod with a ½" (1cm) diameter. You have to bear down hard on the drill to push through the cover, and you will probably have to pull the drill out periodically to clear the hole of paper shreds. Attack one book at a time. Getting a good clean hole through the cover is tricky, because the cover tends to tear. But keep trying and you'll end up with one good one, which is you need. This will be the book that goes on top.

## Making your lamp

✔ Here's the part you can do to impress your friends of an evening: Sit down with all the pieces and assemble.

✔ Before assembling, accommodate the power cord: Open the book that will be on the bottom of your stack and use a razor knife to cut a groove in a section of pages in which the cord will rest (see photo above). If you wish, glue the bottom cover closed to provide a secure base.

# Origami lights

The idea for origami lights came from a friend. I asked her for an idea for decorations for my husband's 50th birthday, and she gave me strings of these beautiful lights. Easy to make, only two ingredients!

—Jane

## Ready, set...

• Most art stores sell many sizes, colors and patterns of origami paper. My favorite size, 3" x 3" (9cm), makes smaller boxes, but beginners may want to start with 4" (10cm) or 4½" (11cm) squares.

• The hardest part is folding the first box. If you have seen origami patterns before, you'll recognize the basic folds. If you can't get all the way to the end, ask a kid. Many of them learn this in school.

• Use patterned papers when available. When combined with a multicolored light string, the effect is luscious. Pair an orange-patterned paper with an orange light, a blue with a blue, and so on.

• I hang multiple strings in the corner of a room, from ceiling to floor, but they will bring cheerfulness or color anywhere you put them. I have left the lights on overnight and sometimes days at a time; the tiny bulbs don't overheat.

## Making your origami lights

✔ Follow the directions here to make as many origami boxes as the number of lights on your string. (For this reason, you may want to use a short string.)

✔ ❶ Fold a square of paper in half vertically and horizontally to make creases. The patterned side of the paper should be on the outside. ❷ With the sheet folded in half once, fold one upper corner down into a triangle. Unfold, and reverse the fold to create a triangle again. ❸ Repeat on the other side to create

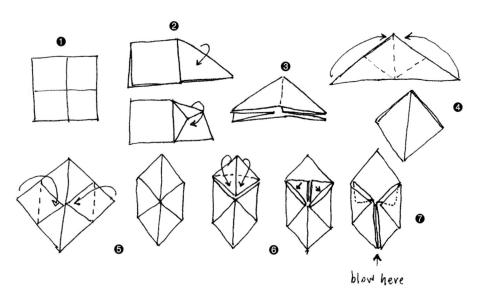

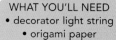

blow here

Ambition Scale

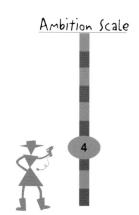

side-by-side layered triangles. ❹ Fold in the outer corners on one side to meet at the upper tip of the triangle. Turn over and repeat. Now you have a diamond. ❺ Fold in the two outer points on one side to the midpoint. Turn over and repeat on the opposite side. ❻ With the top left and top right corners, make two folds each: down once to form a small triangle and down again to slide inside the adjacent pocket. Repeat on the opposite side.

✔ The fun part is blowing the box open. ❼ There is only one opening to the inside. Find it, put your mouth over the hole, and expel one big burst of air. The box will pop open.

✔ Use that same hole to slip the box onto the bulb. The little rim on the socket catches the paper and keeps it from falling off.

# Firefly nightlamp

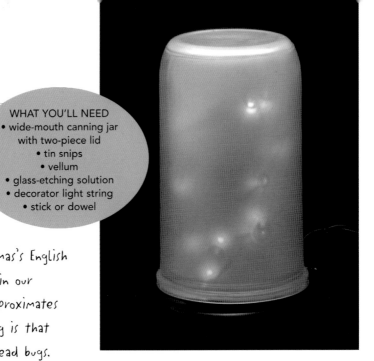

**WHAT YOU'LL NEED**
- wide-mouth canning jar with two-piece lid
- tin snips
- vellum
- glass-etching solution
- decorator light string
- stick or dowel

I grew up in the East, and now, living on the West Coast, I find myself wishing that fireflies had followed me across the Rocky Mountains (also: big, crashing thunderstorms and Thomas's English Muffins, but now the latter have arrived in our grocery stores). Here's a creation that approximates the firefly jars of youth. The silver lining is that you don't wake up to find a jar full of dead bugs.

—Kitty

## Ready, set...

• Choose a short string of lights with twenty or at most thirty-five on the strand. Either a green or white cord is fine. I have used clear, frosted white and even chartreuse bulbs. You can purchase light strings with a "random twinkle," but I have not found anything that approximates the slow flash of the firefly.

• TIP: To frost the jar, use a glass etching product such as Delta's Glass Etching Paint Kit (Air-Dry PermEnamel). This is a nontoxic, nonfume alternative to etching cream, which is essentially an acid and will etch not just the glass but anything else it touches. Delta's etching paint requires two or three coats but is preferable to the hard stuff.

### Ambition Scale

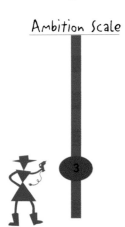

## Making your lamp

✔ Clean the jar thoroughly.

✔ Follow the product instructions to apply a coat of etching paint (a two-part process), and allow to dry.

✔ Using tin snips, cut a notch in the side of the jar lid for the light cord.

✔ Cut a piece of vellum to fit inside the jar so that it covers the sides. You may need to use two pieces.

✔ Apply another coat of etching paint.

✔ Wind the cord of the light string around a stick or dowel cut to fit inside the jar. The cord should be tight around the stick, with the lights splayed outward around it. Leave the plug end of the cord free.

✔ When the jar is dry, place the vellum and the lights inside. Screw the top on, with the plug and cord protruding out the notch. (You won't be able to screw it tight, but that's OK.) Upend, plug in, turn out the lights and pretend it's a summer evening in your favorite meadow.

# Balloon lantern

Make these for any holiday, for parties, to hang around the edge of your porch umbrella in summer. This is a good group project, too; everyone can get messy together.

—Lynn

## Making your lantern

✔ Choose tissue papers according to your desired color scheme. Tear paper into strips about 1" (3cm) wide and 4" (10cm) long.

✔ Mix glue with water to a consistency of thickened milk (approximately two parts glue to one part water).

✔ Blow up a balloon to the size of a large grapefruit. Dip a strip of tissue in the bowl of glue mixture. Use your fingers to squeegee off excess glue. Lay the moistened tissue strip on the balloon. Continue applying wet strips in a random pattern over the balloon, leaving an uncovered circle around the valve. The edges can be ragged, as you will trim off the excess once it is dry.

✔ Overlay papers to create interesting patterns of color. Or, if you want to insert other materials, start with one or two layers of colored tissue over the entire balloon, then apply cut-outs, leaves, or bits of words or poems. Then apply white or light-colored paper as the top layer.

✔ Once you have about three layers of paper on the balloon, place it upside-down on a wide-mouth glass (valve extending downward), to dry overnight.

✔ Pop the balloon and peel it away. Trim around the open edge of your orb so that the opening is at least 4" (10cm)

**WHAT YOU'LL NEED**
- small round balloon
- wide-mouth glass
- tissue paper in various colors
- decorative materials: Japanese maple leaves, fortunes from fortune cookies, haikus printed on strips of paper, clippings from various sources
- tea candle in metal dish
- white glue
- copper tape or ribbon
- copper wire

across. You need to be able to reach in and place a candle inside and provide an opening wide enough to prevent it from burning. Apply a length of copper tape around the rim to finish it off, folding in half lengthwise as you go to cover the inside and outside of the opening. Or glue ribbon around the outside edge.

✔ Punch a hole on either side of the opening and attach a loop of copper wire for hanging.

✔ Place a tea candle contained in a metal dish inside the lantern. Use proper caution as with all open flames; never leave the lantern unsupervised when the candle is lit.

## Ambition Scale

# Sea glass lights

This is one of those projects that was love at first light. I saw a version of these lights bedecking a friend's holiday mantel, but they provide great decorative detail for any season. Although I'm a long-time beach glass collector, I find that buying the glass from a recycling source is a lot more convenient because you need big chunks. Besides, you can get cool pieces like the bottoms of bottles and intact bottle necks. My husband plays the guitar and he found that the bottle necks I bought for this project give him a mean slide.

—Lisa

## Ready, set...

• If you are a beach walker, chances are you already have a jar of sea glass waiting for this project. You can also purchase sea glass by the pound from a number of sources. Collect or purchase more than you'll need, as only the biggest pieces—measuring at least 1½" (4cm) in one direction—will be sufficient for covering the bulbs on a light string.

• You will be using silicone to affix wires to the sea glass. Because you should avoid breathing silicone vapor, it's best to prepare your glass outdoors in advance and leave the assembly for your craft-group gathering.

• Sort through the glass and choose pieces big enough to cover the light bulbs. You will need a piece for each of the lights on the string. Lay out the pieces of glass with the sides you want to see face down. If any pieces are curved, position them so the convex side faces down.

• Cut the copper wire to lengths of approximately 5" (13cm), one for each of the lights on your string. Bend them at the midpoint around a finger, so that they have a hairpin shape.

• Squirt a blob of silicone (bigger than a pea but smaller than a marble) onto a piece of sea glass. Press the curved midpoint of a wire into the blob, so the wire is suspended in the blob's center. Continue until each piece of glass has a wire floating in a silicone blob. Allow to dry overnight.

## Making your lights

✔ Uncoil your string of lights and extend it on the floor or a table. Twist the wire so that all of the light bulbs are aligned in the same direction.

✔ Choose a glass/wire combo and pair it with a light bulb, twisting the copper wire around the light string wire to attach the glass so that it hangs directly in front of the bulb. Continue down the string so that all bulbs are covered.

**WHAT YOU'LL NEED**
• large, colored shards of
sea glass, edges worn smooth
• decorator light string
• copper wire (20 gauge works well)
• silicone rubber sealant

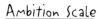
Ambition Scale

5

# Latticework lantern

Who knows where this idea came from. I had to create something for a charity auction with a theme of "lighting a way through the darkness." Close to the deadline I went away to a place with lots of birch trees and a lot of birch bark lying on the ground. One thing led to another...

—Kitty

## Ready, set...

• If you are using electricity to light the lantern, ask for help at the hardware store. You'll need a little instruction (more than we have room for here) in how to set it up. You'll be cutting the female end off an extension cord and wiring it to a socket base. It's easier than it sounds.

• Purchase a few electrical staples at the same time. These are heavy metal staples meant for securing cable; you'll hammer these into place.

Ambition Scale

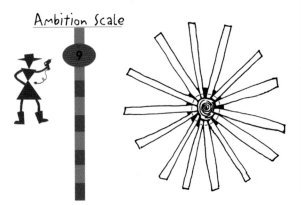

**WHAT YOU'LL NEED**
• lighting fixture: socket base, extension cord and electrical staples; or
• votive candle in small glass jar
• lattice material: sheets of birch bark, scraps of leather or pages from a wallpaper book; you can use any material that has some stiffness and can be cut into strips
• a cross-section of wood, 1" (3cm) thick, sliced off the end of a log roughly 5" (13cm) in diameter
• clothespins or metal binder clips
• staple gun
• glue gun
• adhesive

## Making your lantern

✔ Cut the lattice material into 1" (3cm) strips of 12" (30cm) or longer, depending on the size of your lantern. You will need at least twelve strips.

✔ For an electric lantern, screw the lighting fixture onto the center of the wooden disk. Use the heavy metal staples to secure the cord to the wood. The cord will escape later through a gap in the weaving.

✔ Arrange strips of lattice material around the edge of the wooden disk, overlapping slightly, and use the staple gun to staple them in place.

✔ Take a length of lattice material and, beginning at the base, begin weaving it in and out of the "spokes" attached to the wood. This is where the project gets complicated, because you will be gluing the strip in place as you go and shaping the lantern at the same time. Weave in and out of a few spokes and, holding the horizontal strip in place, stick a dab of hot glue between it and the vertical strip, one after the next. You can reposition them slightly before the glue cools to achieve the shape you desire—whether a bell-shaped curve or a straight cylindrical profile.

✔ Keep working your way up, keeping the weaving fairly tight to give the lantern stability, but not so tight that it lacks small gaps through which the light can shine.

✔ When you've reached the desired height, cut the ends of the spokes so they are even with the top level of weaving. Coat the backs of two more strips of lattice material with glue. Wrap these around the

top edge of the lantern, one on the outside and one on the inside, to give a finished look. Trim off any excess. Clamp in place with clothespins or metal binder clips until the glue dries.

✔ Bend another strip of material into a loose curve; glue each end to the top inside edge of the lantern to create a handle. Glue an additional small strip of material all the way around the inner edge to secure the handle.

✔ If electrical, screw in a light bulb and plug in. If you are using a candle, make sure it sits inside the glass votive holder a safe distance from the lantern handle and sides.

# Single-signature book

I enjoy making books almost as much as I do reading them. I was first introduced to book-making in 1970 in a class in graduate school. Though far outside my major, it became the most important course I took. We deconstructed century-old books and rebound them, made our own marbled paper for endsheets and learned techniques that date back to the Middle Ages and that still produce a well-bound book.

In the years since, I have taught the simple technique presented here to thousands of children and adults in Central and South America, Europe and the U.S. I have introduced book-making in elementary schools, college courses, adult literacy programs, refugee women's centers, book festivals and literary events. Making books has been important in my personal life, too. While living as a teacher overseas, I made small handbound books of "a day in the life" of our children and traded them back and forth with my sisters, who did the same. Since that time, handmade books have marked important occasions for my extended family: the adoption of a child, the loss of a loved one, funny moments of childhood and travels.

Making a book can have a powerful effect on a child. For children who are struggling in school, the process of writing, editing and producing their own books is a transformative experience. Truth be told, I have never made a book with anyone for whom it didn't turn into a magical experience.

—Christine

**Ambition Scale**

5

## WHAT YOU'LL NEED
- paper
- mat board for the covers
- button-strength thread to match the paper color
- photocopies or reductions of favorite photos or other imagery
- cloth or decorative paper (optional)
- clear contact paper (optional)
- sewing needle
- ruler
- tape for spine
- Yes! Paste or glue stick

## Ready, set...

- A good way to obtain mat board at no cost is to take a small box to your local framing store with your name and phone number attached, ask them to save small scraps for you and call you when the box is full.

- Determine the size of the finished book that you desire. (I have made books smaller than the palm of my hand

## CHRISTINE'S BOOKS

*One Night, After It Got Very Dark Outside ...* Here's what happens when the lights stay on in the playroom all night. The stuffed animals get up to all kinds of mischief—swinging from the hanging lamps, ordering pizzas, raiding the refrigerator, taking a bubble bath. But in the morning, they're all back in their places.

*Bringing Ella Home from Chile.* This book commemorates the adoption of our second daughter, from Chile. After I made the book, I made twenty small copies to share with family and friends both in Seattle and Santiago, Chile.

*Grandma Walsh: Her Early Days In Her Own Words.* When my grandmother was ninety years old, I made this book using photos from her childhood and her comments on each of them. I presented Grandma with the original and then made copies for each of my six brothers and sisters for Christmas. Grandma loved showing visitors "her book," and it became a favorite nighttime story for her nineteen great-grandchildren.

*Making an Empanada with Ella and Sylvia in Chile.* This book chronicles a wonderful morning on a trip we took with our girls to South America. It was Ella's first time back to "her" country since her adoption and it was only fitting that she learn how to make one of its wonderful native dishes. The book combines photos, drawings and captions by Ella and some factual information about empanadas.

*Ella and Mommy Finding the Beginning and End of Meridian in the Summer of 1999!* This book celebrates the glory of a summer day when you wake up with nothing to do and say, "Let's have an adventure." Our house is on Meridian Avenue and Ella had always wanted to find out where it began and ended, so we did. We studied a map and found the northernmost end of the road and then drove from there to the southern end, stopping to take photos along the way. Then we wrote a story to go with the pictures.

*Ten Things I Love about [name goes here].* This has become a series for various members of my family. I used small reproductions of photos, magazine cuttings and watercolor paintings to illustrate the reasons I love each of them.

and almost as big as a doorway. The latter weighed five hundred pounds and was in the running for the world's biggest book!) Fold the paper you want to use in half, and then add ½" (1cm) each to the height and width to determine the cover measurements. For example, if you start with standard letter-sized paper stock, which is 8½" x 11" (22cm x 28cm), your finished book will measure 6" x 9" (15cm x 23cm).

• Determine how many pages you want. Remember, the sheets of paper are folded in half, so each sheet equals four pages in the book. Therefore, to make a twenty-four-page book, you will need six sheets of paper. Be sure to allow one sheet of paper for the endsheets and a few pages at the front of the book for a title page preceded by two blank pages. If the book is a gift, it's also fun to include a dedication page and an "about the author" page where you can put your photo or draw a picture of yourself. Don't use more than ten sheets of paper, which will make a thirty-two-page book, or it will be too thick to bind.

• If your book will have text, you have several options: You can handprint your text into a book you have created; you can use a word processing program to write the text, print it out and then cut and paste it into a book you have created; or you can use a program that paginates your text for you (EasyBook by Sunburst is a good example of this type of software), print it out and then create a book from the pages.

• If you want a colorful binding for the cover, use plastic tape in the color you like best. If you don't want the binding tape to detract from the cover design, use clear plastic packing tape. I use 1¾" (4cm) wide tape.

• Decide on the content of your book and gather the necessary photos, images or memorabilia you wish to include.

## Making your single-signature book

✔ Fold sheets of paper in half width-wise to create the signature, or group of pages, of your book. Use a colored, marbled or decorated sheet as the outside page of your signature. When glued into the book this will become the "endsheets" attached to the covers. Be sure to place it with the decorated side facing toward the inside.

✔ Unfold the pages so they lie open, and ❶ attach paper clips at the top and bottom of the outside edges to prevent slipping when sewing.

✔ Use a pencil to mark four evenly-spaced dots along the outside fold (the convex side). These dots will serve as guides for sewing. Measure the width of two fingers at both the top and bottom of the fold and make marks there, and then mark two equally spaced spots between them toward the center of the fold.

✔ Thread your needle with approximately one yard (1m) of thread (this will vary according to the size of the book). Double the thread, but do not tie a knot; just even out the thread so that you have two equal strands. ❷ Make holes by poking the needle through each of the four marks on the fold, piercing through the entire stack of pages.

✔ Insert the needle through the first hole at the top of the paper, on the outer side. ❸ Draw the needle in and out through the next three holes in succession. The needle will emerge on the same side as the one you started on.

✔ Even out the thread so the same amount is at each end and cut the needle off the end. ❹ Bring the two ends together and tie a double knot at the center of

the fold. Cut off the ends of the thread (not too close to the knot or it will come undone). Your signature is now complete and you are ready to bind.

✔ If you want plain mat board covers (which you can decorate later, if you wish), proceed to the next step. Otherwise, cover your mat boards with cloth or decorative paper before binding. Use library paste or white glue spread thin to prevent wrinkling.

✔ Cut a piece of plastic tape that is 2" (5cm) longer than the length of your book and place it sticky side up on your work surface. ❺ Place your boards, cover side down, on the tape, leaving at least a ½" (1cm) of space between the covers, and an equal amount of tape at the top and bottom. Fold the ends of the tape down over the edges of the covers.

✔ Position your signature in the middle of the "spine" so that the exposed stripe of tape will "grab" it. ❻ Use paste to attach the first piece of paper (the first page of your signature) to the inside front cover of your book. Close the book and adjust the fit of the back piece of paper. (If you glue both endsheets down without closing the book first, it may pull too tight and tear when you close it.) Open the book and glue the back endsheet to the inside back cover.

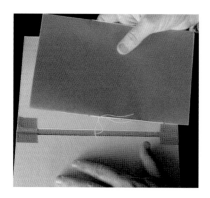

✔ Close the cover and, before the glue sets, adjust the endsheets so the book closes evenly. Decorate the cover and, if you desire, apply a sheet of clear contact paper (cut to size) to protect it. Voilá ... your book is complete!

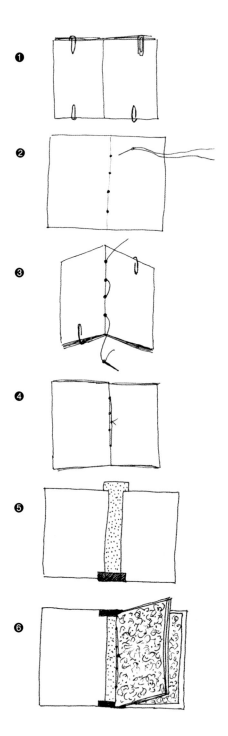

❶
❷
❸
❹
❺
❻

# Collage quilt

We all need our little obsessions, right? At least healthy ones. I began this project during a period of my life when I was fixated on a failed relationship. The preoccupation was getting me nowhere and ruining my mood. So I embarked on a deliberate effort replace it with a focused activity that indulged in another one of my obsessions—cutting up magazines for paper collages. Every time I went into grind mode, I pulled out my scissors and magazines and fell into a blissful state. From the onset I called this paper quilt project "Mindfulness," and if you look closely, you'll see little Buddha images in most of the squares. "Moving On" or "Letting Go" might have been more appropriate titles. And I did.

—Margaret

## Ready, set...

• Gather a stack of magazines, catalogs, brochures, calendars—anything with glossy images. Cut out color swatches, unusual shapes, borders, letters, interesting typography, small images, strips—whatever strikes your imagination.

• I created this quilt square by square, allowing my mood, colors, shapes and serendipity to determine the character of the square. For the most part, I leafed through magazines until an idea, a color scheme or a design leapt out at me. Or I started with one idea and let it grow. An alternative way to approach the project is to determine the patterns ahead of time, as if for a traditional fabric quilt. If you tend to work in a more disciplined fashion, search magazines for the specific colors or shapes you need.

## Assembling your quilt squares

✔ Determine the overall size and layout of your assembled paper quilt. Do you want a square or rectangle? Do you want a vertical or horizontal orientation?

✔ Determine the size of your squares—mine are about 4" (10cm) square—and add at least 1" (3cm) of margin to the height and width to provide spacing between each square once they are assembled. Using a ruler, measure and cut pieces of card stock for backing the squares. With a pencil, draw the outline of the image area onto your squares so that the margins are readily delineated.

✔ Begin by collecting the pieces for your square. You can design it as you go or follow a pattern. Some of my squares are built on strips of color, varied by design. Later in the project, I branched out to a bit freer form. My favorite squares are ones built on images. Once you've found and assembled pieces for a square, play with them a bit. Move them around on the card until you have a design, pattern or image that works.

### Ambition Scale

5

✔ Carefully glue each piece in place. Repositionable glue stick is useful at this stage. You can pick up and replace pieces if they aren't working for you.

✔ Once you've created a desired number of squares, assemble them on the backing you've chosen for your "quilt." Again, play with the layout until it looks just right.

✔ Align the pieces by rows and glue each square down, one row at a time. Use stronger glue, such as Alex Craft Glue, which doesn't cause paper to curl, to attach each square to the backing.

✔ Finish each square with a border, such as peel-stick foil tape, or just let the squares float on the backing.

✔ What do you do with a collaged paper quilt? It's up to you. I framed mine and people love looking at it. But remember, with this project it's as much the doing as the final result. Ohmmmmm.

**WHAT YOU'LL NEED**
- lots of colorful images
- sharp paper scissors
- paper cutter (optional)
- paper or card stock for backing each square
- paper or card stock backing for entire quilt
- adhesive with built-in applicator
- foil tape or other material to frame squares
- glue stick
- ruler

# Real people paper dolls

As kids, my sister and I used to wait impatiently for my mother's *McCall's* magazine to arrive so that we could see the new Betsy doll and her outfits-of-the-month. As an adult, I hit upon an idea while waiting to pick up my photos at the local drugstore. By the cash register there was a cut-out photo of a young girl with a baseball bat, mounted on Plexiglas.

Hmmm, I thought, wouldn't it be great fun for my daughters and their friends to make paper-doll outfits for dolls with their own likenesses? Since then I've thought of making a whole family set of dolls, but I can never get adults to pose in their bathing suits.

—Christine

## Ready, set...

• Have your "model" dress in a bathing suit or underwear and stand in front of a blank wall or other plain background. Take six to eight photos in the typical paper-doll pose: hands slightly extended at sides, palms facing outward, feet a small distance apart, head up. Position yourself directly in front of your subject and kneel down so that your camera is shooting directly at her middle (rather than shooting down at an angle from above). Make sure the feet are in the frame of your shot! For each photo, ask for a different expression: happy, sad, goofy, and so on.

• Develop or print the photos and choose your favorites.

• Take your photos to a copy shop and enlarge on a color copier to the size you desire. From a 4" x 6" (10cm x 15cm) photo, I made 150 percent enlargements for the samples shown. Ask for photo-quality paper, which has a shiny side and is thicker than regular copy paper. Some copy shops carry photo paper in a card stock weight; this is ideal, as you won't have to back the doll with this stiffer paper.

**WHAT YOU'LL NEED**
• color film and camera or digital camera
• paper, colored pencils and decorative
materials for making clothes
• clear contact paper or self-adhesive
laminating sheets (optional)
• manila envelope
• card stock
• Yes! Paste or glue stick

## Making your paper doll

✔ If your color copy is on regular-weight paper, use paste or spray mount to attach the image to a piece of card stock or poster board before cutting.

✔ If you wish, cover the image with clear contact paper or laminating sheet.

✔ Use sharp scissors to carefully cut out your figure.

✔ Present the doll in a manila envelope that will be her home. The doll's alter ego can decorate the envelope to make the home of her dreams.

✔ When making (or explaining how to make) clothes for the doll, don't forget to add the tabs at appropriate spots (shoulders, waist, thighs) to attach the outfits to the doll. You can either create originals or adapt designs from magazines to fit the doll. Wrapping paper provides an endless source of wonderful "fabrics" for the clothing designs.

# Chocolate box valentine

Here's a collaged valentine that will last much
longer than the chocolate that came in the box.
Be it for woman's or man's best friend, it's a true
gift from the heart.

—Lisa

## Ready, set...

• Gather collage materials: clippings of images and words from magazines, wrapping paper or old books, stamped images, dried flowers, tissue paper. Focus on collecting imagery and words that speak to you of *love*. You can also go for the three-dimensional look and gather small plastic figurines to go in your box.

### Ambition Scale

• Remove the chocolate from the box, if you haven't done so already, and eat it as you apply a layer of acrylic paint over both the inside and outside of your box. You can use the lid to make another valentine.

## Making your valentine

✔ Sort through the collage pieces and lay out the ones you intend to use. Begin fitting them into the box, cutting the pieces to size.

✔ Start with the inside of the box "walls." Brush on a coat of collage medium to the first area you want to cover and press on the collage pieces, smoothing from their centers outward. Overlap edges if you wish or leave gaps where the painted surface can show through.

✔ Now cover the inside bottom of the box. Using typical collage techniques, build up several layers of imagery in places to make it more interesting.

✔ Finish with collage materials around the outside of the box. Let all collage pieces dry.

✔ Coat the entire piece with collage medium to seal.

✔ Run a string of glue around the inside edge of the box and press in a string of seed beads. Cut excess bead string after the glue has dried.

✔ Use glue to attach a length of ric-rac around the entire box on the flange. Glue another string of seed beads around the base of the box where the sides meet the flange.

✔ Wrap copper tape around the edge of the box to give it a finished look. String a piece of copper wire for hanging through two holes drilled in the flange. Glue or tape excess wire to the back of the box.

PHOTO

Doña María

Tegucigalpa
Ho

# Embellished frames

A few years ago I used this frame as a craft project for my daughter's eleventh birthday. It was a hit and subsequently migrated to the adults' crafting table.

One of the amusing things about getting this project onto paper has been finding out just how many ways you can describe its featured ingredient: the flat marble! You know—those smooshed pieces of glass that some people put in the bottom of fish tanks or at the bottom of vases. Names we have heard include: half-marbles, flat marbles, cabochons, colored glass blobs and gems. I recently called a Michaels store to invite them to weigh in on the name. Their vote: half-marbles.

Whatever the designation, these are a great addition to any number of craft projects because they slightly magnify anything placed under them, they reflect light and they're beautiful to behold (to this beholder, anyway).

—Camille

**WHAT YOU'LL NEED**
- simple wood frame
- bag of clear glass half-marbles
- white glue
- colored grout
- rubber gloves
- stack of magazines
- acrylic paint

## Ready, set...

• Your frame must have a flat border at least 1" (3cm) wide.

• Take glass and backing out of the frame. Paint the wood with one or more colors.

## Making your frame

✔ Place half-marbles around the frame border with edges touching or spaces between, but don't glue them down yet.

✔ When you have determined the number of half-marbles you will use, find an image or word to go with each. If from a magazine, tear out the page. Place a half-marble over the picture or word you chose and use it as a template for tracing around the image. Then cut out the image, a little smaller than your traced line, so that the resulting cut-out fits perfectly underneath the half-marble with no paper showing around the edge.

✔ Glue your images on the frame with white glue.

✔ Now put a small amount of glue on the back of each of the half-marbles and carefully place them on top of each image. Don't despair if it appears that you'll never see the image through the cloud of white glue. It dries clear and the picture will be visible.

✔ Mix up a small amount of grout and smooth it with your fingers on the exposed wood around each half-marble. Use a wet sponge to wipe off excess grout from half-marbles. Allow to dry according to the grout instructions.

## VARIATION II: FOUND-OBJECT FRAME

I am a pack rat of the highest order. This has resulted in the creation of an array of art projects that give purpose to some of my oddball treasures. Using small objects (usually around a theme) as a border design on a frame is one of these. An example: surround a favorite photo from a trip with small mementos to make the memories even more vivid.

—Lisa

## Ready, set...

• If the frame is plain wood, paint it with a water-based latex paint to provide an interesting background for your objects.

• Gather objects around a theme: a trip, a baby, a family portrait, a graduation picture.

## Making your frame

✔ Remove the glass and backing from the frame so you are working with just the frame structure. Arrange the objects around the frame in an order that pleases you.

✔ Use a glue gun to affix each piece individually.

✔ If you wish, use a sparkle glue applicator to add sparkly swirls around and between objects.

✔ Wash, dry and return glass to the frame. Insert photo and replace backing.

### Ambition Scale

4

**WHAT YOU'LL NEED**
• latex paint (optional)
• plain or painted wooden frame with flat border at least 2" (5cm) wide
• small objects that fit within frame's border
• glue gun
• sparkle glue (optional)

# Dog bone frame

Our dog Argo had long ago graduated to big-dog biscuits when I came across a tin with a few puppy treats left in it. I indulged my nostalgia for his puppy days with this frame. When I showed him the finished project, he liked it so much he tried to eat it. You can adapt this project to celebrate your favorite baby with leftover teething biscuits, precious gum marks intact.

— Kitty

## Making your Frame

✔ Spray both sides of your biscuits with sealant, if you wish.

✔ Mount the photo on a piece of foam core the same size as your photo, using spray mount or an acid-free glue stick. Glue the foam core onto a piece of cardboard substantially bigger than the photo—leaving a margin around the edges of the photo that is wide enough on all sides to affix the biscuits.

**Ambition Scale**

3

✔ Place the biscuits around the photo in whatever artful manner you like. Trace the biscuits with a pencil. Use a craft or razor knife to cut the excess cardboard away from the traced outline, leaving a

**WHAT YOU'LL NEED**
- cardboard
- foam core
- photograph
- biscuits (dog or teething), roughly 1" x 3" (3cm x 8cm)
- spray mount or glue stick
- glue gun
- spray sealant (optional)

backing for your biscuits. If you cut inside the outline by about a ¼" (6mm), the cardboard won't be visible once the biscuits are glued in place.

✔ Glue on the biscuits with a glue gun.

✔ Create an easel to prop up the frame by gluing another dog biscuit onto a strip of cardboard and gluing the strip onto the frame (see photo at right).

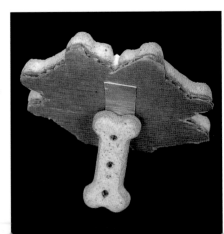

# Stamped mat board

Here's a technique for dressing up a simple frame. It's amazing how you can transform a cheap garage-sale frame by decorating the mat inside it. This works well with a simple photo or art piece. Or you can create some stamped art in contrasting colors and frame it inside your stamped mat.

—Lisa

## Ready, set...

• Precut mats are available at craft and frame stores.

• Use small ink pads like ColorBox Pigment Brush Pads or PaintBox with removable color pads.

• Ask your friends to bring their stamps so you can draw from a combined collection that includes patterns, words, letters and objects.

## Making your mat

✔ Choose ink colors that complement your artwork. Remove the ink pad from its case and use it to apply a layer of colors with brushing motions. Blend several colors for a nice effect (say, yellow to gold to orange). Let dry.

✔ Stamp on black or dark images over the background colors. Try repeating stamps, overlaying stamps and creating patterns, all of which add depth and texture to the color.

✔ That's it! Add art, frame and hang.

## Ambition Scale

3

WHAT YOU'LL NEED
• frame
• white mat board cut to fit frame with an opening cut to fit the photo or artwork
• rubber stamps and stamp ink pads in various colors

PHOTO    93

# BBs in a petri dish

There must be a better name for these little handheld games that test your hand-eye coordination. Roller bearing game? Whatever. Put a face inside and this becomes the rare plastic gee-gaw that kids—and adults—will hang onto.

—Kitty

## Ready, set...

• You can purchase actual petri dishes from a science store or on the Internet. Petri dishes are the right size and shape, but because the lid doesn't attach to the dish, you'll have to add a layer of double-stick foam tape around the inside edge of the lid to secure it. Or you can purchase a plastic dish with a screw-on lid.

• VARIATION: I have also used a plastic bug viewing canister with a magnifier in the lid to give an extra dimension to this project (see photo at top, far right). You can

add a plastic figurine or two as extra obstacles inside the jar, and wrap a message around the outside.

• To make the most creative use of the balls, have the subject of your game pose for the camera in a way that will incorporate the balls. For example, have the subjects pose as if they are juggling, have several arms or are blowing bubbles.

• When you make color copies of your photos, reduce or enlarge to fit the dimensions of the dish.

## Making your game

✔ Trace the dish onto a piece of card stock and a piece of foam core. Cut out both circles, trimming a bit off the edge as you go to achieve a good fit inside the dish.

✔ Using a glue stick or spray mount, attach your image(s) to the paper circle. Glue this onto the foam core circle.

✔ Take a sharp pointy tool—I have used an awl, a nail punch, a ball point pen and a shish kebab skewer—and push some holes into your image to break through the paper and make a slight indentation in the foam core.

✔ Place the circle inside the dish, and add a metal ball for each of the holes.

✔ If you are using a petri dish, add a circle of double-stick foam tape to the inside lip of the lid. Trim off any excess. Work the lid onto the jar so that it is permanently wedged into place.

**WHAT YOU'LL NEED**
• petri dish or plastic dish with screw-off or lift-off lid
• small piece of foam core
• color copies of photos
• small metal balls: BBs, roller bearings or beads
• double-stick foam tape
• glue stick or spray mount

Ambition Scale

5

PHOTO    95

# Copper-edged frame

About ten years ago a few members of our group were invited to the studio of Seattle artist Deborah Mersky for a private art class. One of us had seen her beautifully framed small objets d'art and asked if she would share her secrets. She was only too happy to introduce us to the wonders of copper foil as a craft material. Deborah explained that she had developed the technique as an inexpensive but very impressive framing technique for her small prints.

The following weekend our group headed off for our first getaway weekend where we spent an entire evening and into the wee hours of the morning cutting glass, creating collages and framing. Since that time we have developed many variations—refrigerator magnets, Christmas ornaments, brooches—on the theme that was first explored in Deborah's studio.

—Christine

## Ambition Scale

**WHAT YOU'LL NEED**
- thin pieces of glass (scraps from framing or stained glass suppliers)
- ½" (1cm) copper or silver foil tape (from art or stained glass suppliers)
- thin pieces of mat board or foam core for backing
- images: photos, magazine or calendar pictures, small watercolor paintings
- glass cutting tool
- adhesive
- magnet, pin backing, or copper wire

## Ready, set...

- Because this project involves cutting glass, take some time to practice this technique. Start with a piece of glass that is at least 4" x 6" (10cm x 15cm). Measure, and using a thin-tipped marker, mark a line on your glass where you want to cut it. Practice scoring the glass with your glass cutter, which you hold between your thumb and forefinger. Scoring means making a clean line on the glass, not actually cutting it. Press down fairly hard in order to make the score line. Running the cutter along a straight metal edge lined up along the marker line will help you score a straight line. If your score is deep enough you will be able to take the small ball at the other end of the cutter and tap along the score line, which deepens the fracture. Then hold the glass with one hand on either side of the score line which is on the up side of the glass and gently exert pressure out and down until the glass snaps apart; if all goes well it will make a clean break. "Practice makes perfect" is an adage to keep in mind here. But once you can count yourself among the glass cutters of the craft world, whole new vistas of creativity will open before you.

• Prepare the images you wish to frame. To showcase a photograph, first head to the copy shop and make some reductions. We usually make these images fairly small; a 50 percent reduction of a 4" x 6" (10cm x 15cm) photo works well. Old magazines and calendars are also a treasure trove of possible images.

## Making your frame

✔ Cut a piece of mat board or foam core the exact size of the image you are framing. If you are creating a collage it can be glued on a piece of board as you create it. If you are using a photo, glue it to the board with a light amount of adhesive. A glue stick works well here.

✔ Cut a piece of glass the same size as the image on the board. Clean the piece of glass and place it directly over the image.

✔ Cut a strip of copper foil about ¼" (6mm) longer than the circumference of your piece of glass. Expose about 1" (3cm) of the adhesive backing and begin attaching the exposed foil tape along the edge of the glass/image-board sandwich, centering the tape horizontally so that a small edge of tape extends to either side. Slowly expose the remaining adhesive backing as you apply the tape around the remaining edges. The extra ¼" (6mm) of tape will lap back over where you began. Still holding the piece in your hand, use your thumb to press down the foil on the back of the board.

✔ Lay your piece on a flat surface and carefully fold down the edges of the foil on the glass, one side at a time. One trick is to fold down the two opposing sides and then fold the other two over them, creating symmetrical corners. Don't worry if your foil is a little wrinkled at this point. Grab your handy glasscutter and run the ball along the foil, ironing out the creases.

✔ To create a magnet, glue a magnet onto the back. To create a pin, add a pin backing. To create an ornament or hanging piece, tape a copper wire hanger to the back. You can also hang wire from the bottom to hold beads and other trinkets.

# Five-minute photo albums

As the unofficial photographer and archivist for vacations and celebrations, I often have stacks of photos to send to friends and family members. I used to stick the print doubles in plain envelopes, which just isn't a suitable way to present my photographic talents. It also might explain the "unofficial" in my title. Recently, though, I became inspired by the little photo albums popping up in a variety of stores. I decided to try a few variations using techniques and resources drawn from other projects in this book. It has been great fun creating these fast and easy photo albums that elicit heaps of gratitude from their recipients. With photo corners holding the photos in place, the books can be filled with new photos as desired.

—Christine

### WHAT YOU'LL NEED
- sewing materials
- ribbon
- adhesive photo corners
- colored card stock for cover
- paper for interior, color and weight as desired
- scissors
- mat knife
- paper cutter (optional)
- long-arm stapler (optional)
- hole punch (optional)
- gift box (optional)

## Ready, set...

- Choose a set of photos to feature in the album. I usually include between ten and twenty images, one photo per page. For twenty photos, I cut five strips of paper. The instructions that follow give dimensions for books holding 4" x 6" (10cm x 15cm) photos.

- Choose pieces of card stock for the cover and the inside pages.

## Making your bound album

✔ For the cover cut a piece of card stock 14" (35cm) long by 5" (13cm) wide. Using a mat knife, make a light score down the center and fold in half so the cover measures 7" x 5" (18cm x 13cm).

✔ For the interior pages cut 14" x 5" (35cm x 13cm) strips of paper. Fold these in half. Place the folded cover around the interior pages to make sure that the paper is aligned. Then unfold the papers to bind.

✔ BINDING VARIATIONS: ❶ Using a long-arm stapler, staple the pages and cover along the folded seam with two evenly spaced staples. ❷ Holding the cover and pages in one hand, use a hole punch to make a hole about 1" (3cm) from each the top and bottom of the cover seam. If the paper is too thick, punch holes through each piece individually. Thread a ribbon through the holes and tie off in a bow on the outside of the cover. ❸ Use the instructions for the single-signature book on pages 78-81.

✔ OPTIONAL FINISHING TOUCHES: ❶ Use adhesive photo corners to place photos in the album. ❷ Cut out a small window and tape in a small reduction of one of the photos. ❸ Cut two 5" (13cm) lengths of ribbon. Tape one piece to the inside of the front cover and one to the inside of the back cover so a length of about four inches hangs off each cover. Use these to tie the book closed. ❹ Cut a 4" x 5" (10cm x 13cm) piece of paper and affix to the insides of both the front and back covers to conceal the taped ribbon ends and/or the back of the inset photo.

## Making your accordion album

✔ Cut a long strip of paper to accommodate the number of photos you will include. For example, to display ten 4" x 6" (10cm x 15cm) photos, you'll need a strip of paper 5" x 35" (13cm x 89cm). You probably will have to glue two or more strips together, leaving a bit of extra on each end, to make one long enough.

✔ Fan fold the strip and use adhesive photo corners to place the photos, one per page, between the folds.

✔ Use a decorative gift box to hold the accordion album, or cut card stock or mat board and glue to the each end of the accordion to make it more sturdy.

Ambition Scale

# photo mosaic

Like most of us, you probably have boxes and envelopes filled with photos that never made it into a
scrapbook or merited a frame. Here's a creative use of
these "outtakes" that can be applied to a range of
projects. Once you create the photo "tiles," you can
do something quick and simple, such as decorating
the cover of a journal, tray or box lid, or be more
ambitious and create a one-of-a-kind tabletop.

—Kay

## Ready, set...

• Gather an assortment of photos around a
certain theme. For example, you can use outtake
photos from a trip to create a special photo
journal commemorating the trip's highlights.
The discerning viewer will be able to discover
memorable spots captured in the photo pieces.
Another idea: Make a collection of squares that
have entire or partial faces in them, and use these
to build a pattern.

- Create a template for cutting photos into 1" (3cm) squares, strips or diamond shapes. The template will enable you to trace a uniform shape for cutting. To create templates, use scraps of mat board or thin cardboard, or purchase a plastic template of shapes from an art supply store. If you measure carefully, you can skip the template and cut the images with a craft knife and ruler.

- Cut out lots of shapes from the photos and sort them by color and shading.

## Making your mosaic

✔ Design a pattern using repetitions of colors and/or content. You can use books of quilting patterns for inspiration.

✔ To create a cover for a journal or book, mount pieces directly onto the covers. Use paste or photo adhesive to affix the mosaic pieces. When finished, paint a thin coat of a polymer medium (e.g., Mod Podge) over the surface to protect it.

✔ VARIATION: For a tabletop, cut a template the exact size of the tabletop out of thick paper, and design your photo mosaic to fit. Then glue the finished design, piece by piece, to the paper with photo adhesive. When you are done, apply two coats of sealant to protect the surface from spills and scratches, or place it under a piece of glass cut to fit.

**Ambition Scale**

4

**WHAT YOU'LL NEED**
- scrap photos
- template material
- backing material
- craft knife
- cutting mat
- metal ruler
- adhesive
- sealant

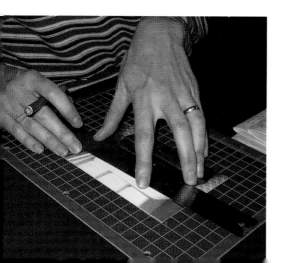

PHOTO 101

# Vine lampshade

This project originated with some lampshades my daughter saw while traveling in South Africa. I was trimming some grapevines and decided to recreate the shades for her as a birthday gift. We made the support for the shades with copper plumbing hardware—but that's another story.

—Phyl

## Ready, set...

• You can find metal frames for making your own lampshades at some lighting supply stores or online. The frame I used is 9" (23cm) wide at the top and 12" (30cm) wide at the base. I wouldn't recommend a shade much smaller than this because it will be more difficult to wind the vine in and out.

• When purchasing the metal base for your shade, decide whether you want a hanging or table lamp. Then purchase the appropriate hardware.

• I used grapevines, but any woody vine will work. Cut off the side shoots, leaving the curlicue strands the vine uses for climbing; these make the shade more interesting. Cut off the ends of each vine, if necessary, to remove thick and thin portions. Your aim is to work with vines that are thin enough to weave fairly easily, yet thick enough to fill in and look substantial.

## Ambition Scale

8

## Making your shade

✔ Apply matte brown spray paint to the entire metal frame to camouflage it.

✔ Soak the vines in water for an hour or longer until they're flexible enough to wrap around the frame. Keep the vines in the water as you work, pulling them out one at a time as needed; they dry out quickly.

✔ Start weaving around the bottom of the frame and work your way up, winding the vine over two or three supports at a time, then behind another support to secure it, then back out and around a few more supports. This maximizes the coverage outside of the frame. Keep pushing the vine down toward the larger, bottom ring of the frame to keep the weaving as tight as possible.

✔ When you come to the end of a vine, leave plenty of extra on the inside of the frame. Wedge it into place with the length of new vine above it.

✔ If any of the spray paint rubbed off during weaving, use brown acrylic paint and a toothpick or brush to touch up the spots where metal is visible.

# Fairy chairs

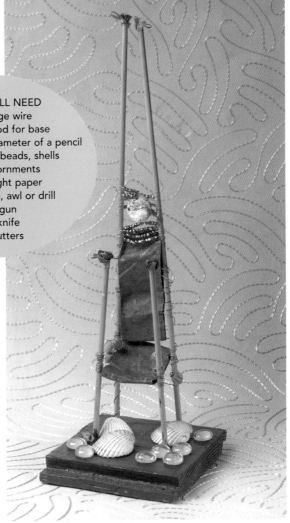

VARIATION I: STICK CHAIR

A few years back my daughter Ella took a summer art class from Cynthia. She spent a week exploring the world of fairies through art projects. Without a doubt, her favorite creation was a fairy chair. The fairy she made fair the chair was lost in a move, and I have since taken over ownership of the chair as a favorite resting place for my Numero Uno Spirit Doll. What special treasure needs a chair in your household?

—Christine

**WHAT YOU'LL NEED**
- thin-gauge wire
- block of wood for base
- dowel about the diameter of a pencil
- assortment of beads, shells or other adornments
- heavy-weight paper
- leather punch, awl or drill
- glue gun
- craft knife
- wire cutters

## Ready, set...

• Gather all of your materials and decide on the size of your chair. This will be determined by the measurements of the fairy, spirit doll or other creature for which it is intended. For the sample shown, the two longer sticks measure about 10" (25cm) and the two shorter ones about 5" (13cm).

• Get a small block of wood that will hold the chair plus about 2" (5cm) of border on all sides.

### Ambition Scale

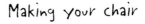

5

## Making your chair

✔ Mark four spots on the block of wood for the legs of the chair. Use a sharp implement (a leather punch, awl or drill) to bore four small holes into the wood. Put one stick into a hole at a time, and use a hot glue gun to cement it into place.

✔ To create a seat and backrest, use thin-gauge wire to lash sticks together, weave a wire mesh seat and back and insert paper for your "upholstery" or string tiny seed beads on a wire framework. Cut a small notch in the outside of each of the legs at the seat height, and wrap wire around the notches to attach the seat to the legs.

✔ VARIATION: Weave, fasten or glue additional decorations such as feathers, tiny shells or beads to the back and sides of your chair.

✔ Paint and decorate the block of wood to fit the design of the chair.

Ambition Scale

8

VARIATION II: TWIG CHAIR

Having long admired deck furniture made of found wood at my aunt's camp in Nova Scotia, I decided to make a tiny version of the same design. When you stick a miniature chair like this alongside a path or on a stump, a young child will discover it and believe that elves and goblins do exist.

—Phyl

## Ready, set...

• Gather different sizes of twigs. The best kind for the back and seat of the chair are alder, willow and red osier because of their pliability. Include twigs that are covered with lichens if you like the look.

• Gather all of your materials and decide on the size of your chair. The example shown is less than 6" (15cm) tall.

WHAT YOU'LL NEED
• plenty of twigs
• lichens and other natural adornments (optional)
• glue gun
• wood glue
• craft knife
• fishline
• toothpicks

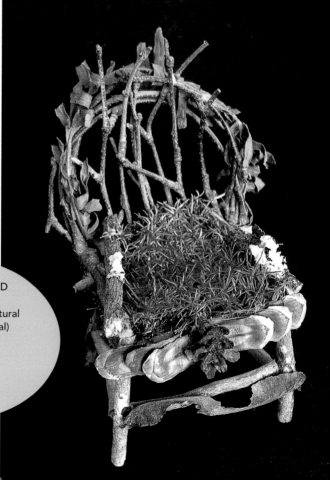

## Making your twig chair

✔ Start by building the bottom frame of the chair—the legs and the cross-supports. For the legs, cut four twigs of the same diameter to the same length. Then cut seven cross pieces—four for the sides, two slightly longer ones for the front and one slightly shorter than the side supports for the back.

✔ Apply hot glue to each end of the two front cross pieces and hold them against the two front legs until they stick solidly.

✔ Do the same with the shorter back cross piece and back legs.

✔ Join the frame together by gluing the four side cross pieces in place between the front and back leg pieces.

✔ Measure the correct length for the arms and cut. Glue them across the top ends of the four legs. This will help to stabilize the frame.

✔ Tie the fishline around any joint that you feel needs added stability. Using a toothpick, spread wood glue around each joint for reinforcement.

✔ Place a crosspiece on the top back part of the frame (on the inner side of the back legs) to support the seat.

✔ For the chair back, twist together two longer pliable twigs, bend them into a U shape, and glue them to the lower back part of the frame with a glue gun. Tie them in place with the fishline and add wood glue.

✔ Use a glue gun to glue pliable, thinner twigs in three places: the top front and back crosspieces and the top of the chair back. Again, tie fishline to hold wherever necessary and add wood glue.

✔ Allow the glue to dry overnight. Then cut off the fishlines.

✔ Now comes the fun part—glue on the lichens and mosses, which happily cover mistakes and make your creation look like a true woodland fairy's chair.

# Leaf lampshade

At the dump on an island in Puget Sound there is something called The Store, where everything is free. On each and every visit I have found the most amazing things, including a nice old lamp with a stained shade and a big plastic bag filled with hundreds of bay leaves. You can guess the rest of this story.

—Kitty

## Ready, set...

• You usually can buy bay leaves at a reasonable price where bulk herbs and spices are sold. Bay costs about sixteen dollars a pound in Seattle, but it doesn't weigh much—three dollars will buy you enough for a medium-sized lampshade. Be sure to buy more than you think you'll need because you'll have to sort through to find the whole ones. Save the broken ones for your spice drawer.

Ambition Scale

4

## Making your lampshade

✔ Sort through the leaves and make a pile of the whole ones.

✔ Put a dab of hot glue onto the back of a leaf and stick it onto the bottom of the shade with the tapered bit hanging beyond the edge. Continue placing leaves around the bottom edge, overlapping a bit and letting the tips hang so they cover the shade completely. Once you have gone all the way around the bottom edge, begin the next row. Glue the leaves in the alternate spaces so that the tips extend into the gaps formed by the tops of the leaves in the row below—as if you were tiling a rooftop. Caution: it is easy to burn yourself with hot glue as you handle the leaves—take care!

✔ Proceed row by row all the way to the top, extending the tops of the leaves slightly above the top edge and overlapping them slightly to hide the shade.

# Shell box

Our family loves taking trips to the ocean. Many of the beach treasures we bring home are left in plastic bags in the midst of camping gear and aren't found until the next time we head to the coast. Often, it is the smell that alerts us to their location! I created these personalized shell boxes for my children to make use of our shell collections and to provide reminders of the ocean during those long winter months.

—Lisa

**WHAT YOU'LL NEED**
- shells and beach glass
- simple pinewood box or cigar box
- glue gun or other adhesive of your choice
- paint for box

## Ready, set...

- Gather more beach materials than you think you will need. Decorate only the lid or the entire box. Use your collected beach finds, though there's nothing wrong with purchasing extras at the craft store. Strings of shells from the store are perfect for spelling a name on the box lid.

- Paint your box and lid with a glossy or matte latex or acrylic paint. I used sea blue as an appropriate background color.

## Making your shell box

✔ Use a string o' shells or individual pieces to spell out a name, and then create a design around it. It is a good idea to lay out your shells and glass in a rough approximation of your final design before you start gluing them down. Use clusters of shells and glass in the four corners to highlight the name in the middle.

✔ Use your glue gun to affix shells where you desire.

✔ If you want to cover your entire box with shells, make sure to leave space uncovered where the lid drops down over the box.

Ambition Scale

5

# gift cards

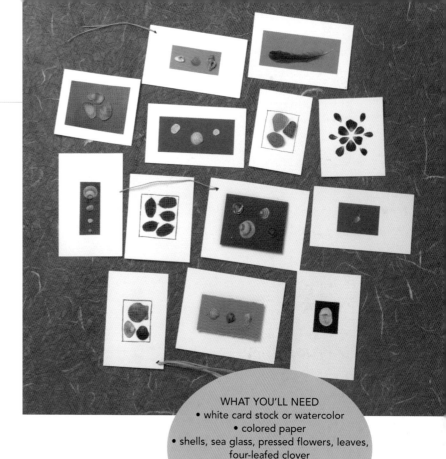

Let's turn for a moment to the subject of wrapping presents. We may be creative types with fine aesthetic sensibilities, but there are more important things in life than worrying about elaborate gift packaging. I say, throw the present in a bag and let a nice handmade tag make up for the brown paper wrapping. Better yet, make a bunch of tags and keep them around for attaching to a completely naked bottle of wine, jar of jam, diamond necklace, etc. as needed.

—Kitty

## Ready, set...

• For the background color: color-saturated papers as opposed to construction paper, works best. Whenever I have a house painting project, I inevitably gather many color sample cards and then stash them away (they're too beautiful to pitch). Here's a perfect use for them. I also use swatches of paper samples that printers often give to graphic designers and other clients.

## Making your gift cards

**WHAT YOU'LL NEED**
• white card stock or watercolor
• colored paper
• shells, sea glass, pressed flowers, leaves, four-leafed clover
• white glue
• ribbon or raffia
• paper cutter, optional

✔ Cut white card stock to your preferred size. A paper cutter makes fast work of this.

✔ Cut color panels to a size slightly smaller than the white card, and glue on.

✔ Apply a thin bead of white glue to the edge of each shell, or over the back of flat petals, leaves or sea glass. Affix to the card.

✔ Cut a small triangular hole (or use a small hole punch if you have one) in a corner. Thread through and tie on a piece of ribbon or raffia for tying the card to your gift.

## Ambition Scale

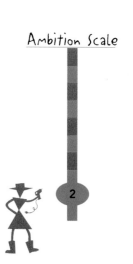

2

# Adirondack birdhouse

If you are a collector of forest flotsam, as I am, perhaps you will welcome a project that uses it to create a beautiful home for a bird family.

—Kitty

## Ready, set...

• Purchase an unadorned wooden or heavy paperboard birdhouse, available at craft stores.

• Gather a few bags of natural materials: sticks of various thicknesses, several types of pine cones, lichen, dried fungus, bark. It's important to have a lot of material from which to pick and choose because it goes only a little way when you are layering on the birdhouse.

**WHAT YOU'LL NEED**
- plain birdhouse
- natural materials
- glue gun and lots of glue cylinders
- garden clippers

Ambition Scale

7

✔ VARIATION: You can get ambitious and do a bigger version, such as this kindling box with a different design on each side.

## Making your birdhouse

✔ If you are a design-in-advance person, sketch a design for each of the sides, the roof and the bottom of the house. Then assemble piles of the natural materials you will need to achieve the design for each portion of the house. If you are a design-as-you-go person, lay out all of your materials and sort according to type so that you can grab as you glue.

✔ Cut sticks to frame the edge of each side of the house, and use hot glue to affix them. Then use a range of materials to fill in the space inside the sticks, using plenty of hot glue to secure each piece. Your designs can be as simple or elaborate as you like. When you finish a side, use scissors to trim off all the glue filaments dangling here and there.

✔ Cut sheets of bark to cover the roof, or piece it together from several bark chunks, allowing some to hang over the roof edges a bit. Or use the individual "tag" pieces from pine cones as roofing tiles; starting at the bottom edge of the roof, glue the tiles on one row at a time. If you wish, glue a strip of bark across the pinnacle where the tiles meet.

✔ Tuck some loose nesting material here and there so the birds don't try to pull the glued material off the outer walls. Don't use synthetic fibers.

## A note about providing birdhouses

Due to loss of habitat, light pollution, acid rain, pesticides and predation from a house cat population run rampant, the U.S. songbird population has gone into steady decline. Some species have diminished by 90 percent over the last fifty years. No matter how you look at it, these birds are stressed. It's helpful for them to have safe housing during breeding periods; ready access to a home means birds can get on with the important business of making more birds. But it's important to know that different birdhouse models attract different birds (from up to fifty cavity nesting species, depending on where you live), and you want to provide homes for the birds that need it, not opportunistic and invasive species like starlings. For success in attracting a particular type of bird, look for Web sites or get a book to learn about the size of hole for the birdhouse, where to locate it and how to care for it. Seeing birds move into your birdhouse is a soul-satisfying experience.

# Island in a box

Use this project to memorialize any special place that is your own personal "island." Here is how it originated: For many years, members of my family have spent a summer week or two at an aunt's cabin on a lake in Nova Scotia. The lake is large and peppered with tiny islands that boast a few trees and some vegetation. Long ago, my nature-loving and clever aunt offered us a deal: We could each "claim" an island if we could canoe to it, get onto it, walk around its perimeter and clear a path through the brush from end to end. Each summer we had to repeat this to keep the claim alive. The advertised reward was the right to name the island and draw it in on a map of the lake, but the real reward, we now realize, was time spent getting to know a small patch of land intimately, with all its plants and bugs and rocks and dirt that became precious because they were "ours"

alone. A few summers ago I created boxes for various family members with images of their islands and things I'd gathered from each. This involved a fair amount of canoeing and enabled me to report back on who had fallen behind on their island upkeep.

This project doesn't require an island, of course; it can be applied to any patch of land near and dear to your heart including a meadow, a patch of forest, even a city park.

—Kitty

## Ready, set...

• Craft stores sell plain brown boxes in a variety of shapes and sizes, ready and waiting for you to transform them. I used a box with a solid lid attached at the back to swing open. Notice that these can also be shelved like a book. You also can purchase a box with a framed opening on the lid, into which you can slide a photo. Cigar boxes also work for this project.

• Gather any souvenirs that are meaningful to you or to the giftee. Natural materials could be a rock or two, a chunk of bark from a special tree, a piece of moss or lichen, dragonfly wings, dried turtle eggshells, leaves or flowers that you can dry or press. Other souvenirs might include shells, ferry ticket stubs, little sketches, beach finds, wine labels, kitschy mementos—anything that gets you a little misty-eyed about your favorite place.

**WHAT YOU'LL NEED**
• box with hinged lid
• photos or color copies of photos
• acrylic paints and/or collage materials
• souvenirs
• essential oil or scent
• small plastic magnifier
• adhesive

## Making your box

✔ Paint your box inside and out with an impressionistic pastiche of colors. Leave the contents of the box a surprise, or paint a title (such as "____'s Place") on the lid.

✔ Glue an image on the inside of the lid.

✔ Attach a piece of cord to the magnifier handle, and tape it to one of the inside walls of the box.

✔ Fill the box with the souvenirs. If there's a scent that reminds you of the place, you can sprinkle it on a piece of moss or lichen so that each time you open the box you get a waft of cedar, lavender or fir, for example.

### Ambition Scale

6

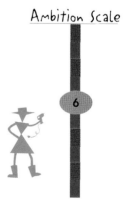

# Window painting

Painting on glass is a fun challenge, because you have to go about it backwards. It's refreshing to do something counterintuitive every once in a while. We had some old windows that I decided to use for practicing painting on glass. I ended up painting the numbers of our street address and hanging it on our house. Soon thereafter a friend suggested I send a photo of it to *Sunset* magazine as an entry in a contest about unique ways of posting your address numbers on your home—and dang if I didn't receive a check from them for a hundred dollars.

—Kitty

## Ambition Scale

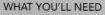

**WHAT YOU'LL NEED**
- acrylic paints
- old window with wooden frame
- paintbrushes
- single-edge razor blade
- eye hooks and picture wire
- spray sealant

## Painting your window

✔ Clean the window. With a dark crayon, sketch a design on the glass on the front side of the window. Then use the crayon to shade in the parts of the design that will be in the foreground. These typically will be the areas of shadows and highlights, as well as dark outlines of lighter objects.

✔ Flip the window over and paint the shaded areas first. For the example shown at left, my first layer included the numbers and highlights and shadows of the additional elements (sky, mountains, flowers).

✔ When the first layer of paint is dry, paint the next layer, the main colors of each of the objects.

✔ Then finish up with the final layer(s): the overall background.

✔ You can apply more color nuances to the painting by scratching through a layer of paint with the razor blade; then apply another color over the scratch marks.

✔ Use the razor blade to scrape off any areas that don't work out, and start again.

✔ Spray one or two coats of sealant over the finished painting.

✔ To hang the window, screw an eye hook two thirds of the way up each side of the frame and run picture wire between them.

# Portable shrine

This project is a wonderful example of a cross-fertilization process that some-times takes place between groups. About five years ago, I dropped in for a visit with Women Who Run with Glue Guns, where Lynn introduced me to tin-box art. I took the idea back to my group and we have been working with this rare art form ever since.

With my Catholic upbringing, I am fond of creating shrines with glow-in-the-dark Virgin Marys and nun figures. I have produced shrines to "Our Lady of Perpetual Study" (for a friend who was studying for her medical boards) and "Our Lady of Unending Equity" (for a friend who was getting a job as a social worker). One of our group's most unusual shrines was the one Sarah made for her father who had lost parts of two fingers in a bandsaw accident. Sarah made a shrine to the missing fingers by creating two fingers out of Fimo, gold-leafing them, and surrounding them inside the shrine with images of hands.

—Christine

## Ready, set...

• Altoids boxes must have been invented with this project in mind, though other mint tins in various shapes and sizes work also.

• This project is a perfect example of the benefits of keeping an ongoing collection of found objects that can eventually find their way into a project. Photos, magazine clippings and fortune cookie messages make good collage materials for the "walls" of your box; plastic figures play up the three-dimensional aspect. You can also mount photos on foam core and cut them out to give them depth.

Ambition Scale

5

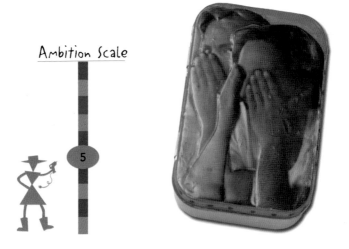

## Making your art tin

✔ Clean the tin and coat inside and out with spray paint. You can use any color you like. Gold, silver, and black are good base colors.

✔ Use your adhesive(s) of choice to attach decorative materials to the interior and exterior of the tin.

✔ A good way to attach a small object (such as a plastic figure) inside the shrine is to glue a small magnet onto the base or the back of the item, and then place it in position. You can then remove it or move it around if you want a change of scenery in your box.

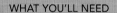

**WHAT YOU'LL NEED**
• tin box with a hinged lid
• decorative materials: glitter, sequins, small shells, clippings, photos
• spray paint
• adhesive
• small magnets (optional)

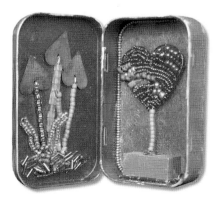

# Matchbox serenity garden

## Ambition Scale

Any time is a good time to quiet your mind. Late for a meeting and stuck at a red light? Waiting in the doctor's examining room for someone to remember you're there? Need a distraction near your computer? Take a few seconds and rake your garden. Breathe deeply. Imagine you are a teeny, tiny person sitting cross-legged at the garden's edge. Breathe deeply again. Imagine you are an infinitesimal grain of sand in your garden. (Don't breathe too deeply or you may blow the sand out of your garden.) Feel better?

—Christine

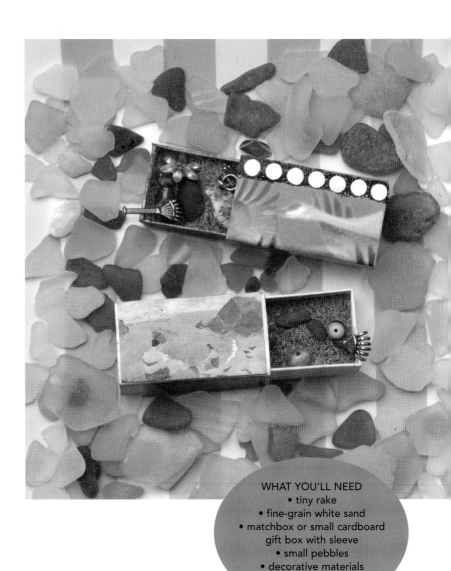

WHAT YOU'LL NEED
- tiny rake
- fine-grain white sand
- matchbox or small cardboard gift box with sleeve
- small pebbles
- decorative materials
- paints

# Ready, set...

• The ideal matchbook size is about 2" x 1" (5cm x 3cm), though some people prefer a larger box. We have found that matchboxes from cigar stores are the sturdiest. You can use a big box of matches or even a cigar box if you want a big garden, but a truly zen-inducing portable garden should be small.

• Another option: You can buy small, white gift boxes from a box/packaging distributor, which give you a nice, blank surfaces to work with, However, we found we had to slide the box back and forth in its case repeatedly to get it to open with ease. If the casing around your box has a tight fit, don't paint the inside box, which will make the box that much harder to open and close.

• Find the finest-grain white sand available. Look at a sand and gravel supplier, home improvement store or pet store. You can usually find small bags of fine sand wherever aquarium fish are sold. Before purchasing, ask for a sample so you can be sure it is fine enough for creating a pattern with a rake.

• Every serenity garden needs a rake. This can be hard to find when you need one 1" (3cm) or smaller. Bead stores sometimes stock these in their charms sections.

• Gather small pebbles as the "boulders" for your garden. (This is a good excuse for an outing to a beach or lakeside, where you can pretend to be a Buddhist monk studying the inherent perfection of each stone.) Bring home a bag of pebbles, rinse them in a colander and sort into like sizes.

# Making your serenity garden

✔ Paint the surface of the matchbox and its sliding cover with acrylic paint.

✔ VARIATIONS: Choose from a variety of media and decorative materials to embellish the casing for your garden. For example, you can: ❶ make a photocopied reduction of a photo and glue it onto the top of the box, ❷ paint or decorate the outer sides, ❸ create a collage of images on the top and sides of the box around a "serene" theme, ❹ do a miniature watercolor and affix to the box top or ❺ create a three-dimensional assemblage of items on a painted box.

✔ Fill the matchbox a third of the way with sand and add one or two pebbles. Remember, less is more; you'll need space to make patterns with the rake. Store your rake inside the box.

# Matchbox homage

This project is a variation on the Matchbox Serenity Garden, but here you are creating a tribute to a friend, family member or even your personal hero/heroine. These make a wonderful birthday gift for someone special. The only question is, once you've given someone her own personal homage, what do you give her next year?

—Christine

## Ready, set...

• When you've decided on the person or theme you wish to celebrate with the box, make a small color reproduction of a favorite photo of the honoree as the design base of the box top. Remember, the color copier is your best friend for projects like this one. If your photograph measures 4" x 6" (10cm x 15cm), reduce it by 50 percent to achieve a typical matchbox size, about 2" x 1" (5cm x 3cm). At some copy shops you have the option of repeating the image to fill the sheet with no difference in cost. I use the extras to do "practice runs" with my design ideas until I find the one I like or as components in other projects, such as tiny books.

## Making your matchbox homage

✔ See the "Matchbox Serenity Garden" description notes on the previous page. Follow the advice on obtaining and preparing your matchbox.

✔ Glue the photo of your honoree to the top of the box. Use small glitter pens to create a border design around the image and, if you desire, sequins as a border around the outer edge.

✔ Once the outside of the box is decorated to your satisfaction, turn your attention to the contents. Some examples of items that I have included are: charms, Mexican milagros, Guatemalan "worry dolls" (the kind that come as a set in a small box at most import stores), a short poem rolled up into a tiny scroll, a favorite bead; a tiny angel (or devil), a shell, a short note of appreciation for the honored friend. You get the picture—there are endless possibilities.

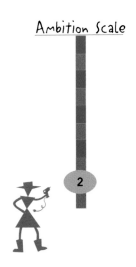

Ambition Scale

2

WHAT YOU'LL NEED
- matchbox
- decorative materials
- special objects
- paints
- photo
- glitter pens

# Faux tooled silver

I have admired the beautiful work of Mexican artisans, their handtooled silver creations in particular. The following projects have their genesis in appreciation of this craftsmanship, using a variation on both the materials and technique used in the traditional craft. Nothing but respect for the originals is intended!

—Sarah

Ambition Scale

4

**WHAT YOU'LL NEED**
- mat knife
- embossing tool
- very thin (⅛"/3 mm) sheets of foam board
- roll of aluminum metal embossing foil
- spool of medium-gauge wire
- permanent ink markers
- metal-edged ruler
- Scotch tape
- cardboard
- duct tape

VARIATION I: PLAQUE

## Ready, set...

• A word on materials: An embossing tool is a tool with a rounded point for etching designs into the embossing foil. It usually comes packaged with the foil. The foil and tool can be purchased at craft stores or online. Look for thin sheets of foam board ⅛" (3mm) thick. These often are available in packages of ten, also through craft retailers.

• If you feel unsure about drawing your own border designs, find a book at the library that has photos of handtooled designs and adapt some of them for your frame border.

## Making your plaque

✔ Decide on a shape for your plaque. It can be square, rectangular or any shape that suits your fancy. Measure and cut the foam board and embossing foil as for the frame (see next page), but without cutting a center opening.

✔ Place the foil on top of the foam board and create mitered corners as with the frame. Fold back the cut portions and fasten with tape. To make a neat fold on curved edges, cut slits every ½" (1cm) and then fold the pieces one at a time, in sequence, over onto the foam board and secure with tape.

✔ Emboss designs on the plaque. You can reserve the center for writing a special message.

✔ Finish the back by attaching cardboard with duct tape.

# Making your frame

✔ Decide on both the outside and inside dimensions of your frame. You want the frame to be at least 2-3" (5-8cm) wider in both height and width than your photo or print. You can then add an extra inch or two to the bottom edge to lift the framed image higher in the frame. When you take the measurements for the opening for your photo, make the opening slightly smaller than the photo's dimensions so no margin shows.

✔ Mark lines for the outside edges of the frame on the foam board and use a ruler and mat knife to cut out the shape. Now carefully measure the opening for the photo or print. Use the ruler and mat knife to cut the opening.

✔ Unroll the aluminum embossing foil and cut off a piece 2" (5cm) bigger than the frame's overall width and height.

✔ Center foil on top of the foam board frame. Use the mat knife, to cut off each corner of the foil close to but not quite touching the foam board. Fold the excess over to the back of the foam board and fasten with Scotch tape.

✔ Very carefully cut an X across the middle of the opening for your photo, starting each of the cuts at a corner and slightly within the inside border of the frame. Fold the edges through the inside of the frame around to the back of the foam board and tape.

✔ Now you are ready to emboss. Use your embossing tool to etch a design into your silver frame. Press hard enough to make a groove in the foam, but not hard enough to rip the foil. Have fun with your designs!

✔ If you want to add a little color, use a permanent marker to fill in some of your etched lines.

✔ Carefully center the photograph in the opening and tape in place. Back the whole frame with a piece of cardboard cut to fit. Use the duct tape to "finish" the back of the frame, covering up loose ends, the cardboard backing and the exposed foam board.

✔ Cut a small piece of wire and bend it into a U shape. Invert the U and use a small piece of duct tape to fasten it at the top of the frame. This will provide the hook for hanging your work.

# Tin art

A few years back I was really into metalsmithing, but after becoming pregnant, I decided it was just too toxic an activity and began exploring other avenues for creating metal art. I took a class in tinwork at a local art studio and have been hooked on it ever since. I have been amazed at how similar it is to other crafting projects that use the basic cut-and-paste methods, the only difference being a rivet gun and hammer instead of a glue gun.

—Sarah

**WHAT YOU'LL NEED**
- decorative tins
- upholstery or ball peen hammer
- small copper or brass nails or tacks
- wooden base object
- tin snips

## Ambition Scale

5

## Ready, set...

• Become a tin hound by scavenging local thrift stores and garage sales for cast-off cookie and candy tins of old. Also keep a sharp eye out for tin cans with color images printed directly on the metal (as opposed to those with paper labels); coffee cans are good examples. There seems to be a welcome trend in packaging items in tin once again, so your search may be easier than you think.

• Using your tin snips, cut apart your tins or containers. Look for designs or patterns that you want to use and cut them out just as you would images on paper. Have a variety of sizes and colors of tin scraps assembled before you start your tin art.

• Choose a wooden object to use as the base for your tin art. This could be a scrap piece of wood, a sturdy wooden frame with smooth surfaces, a cigar box, a shadow box or almost any other wooden object.

## Making your tin art

✔ Use basic collage techniques to create your designs. Begin by placing your first piece of tin on the wooden surface and use your small hammer and the nails of your choice to fasten it to the wood. Make sure the nails do not go all the way through the wood. You may need to shorten the nails; if so, use a sturdy wire cutter, cutting on the diagonal (so they'll still be pointy) to the desired length. Of course, it would be a whole lot easier to get the short nails in the first place, so take a trip to the hardware store and ask for the right nail for the wooden object you are decorating.

✔ Layer your pieces of tin to create a design of your liking, hammering each piece down as you go. As in collage, start with background pieces first and build up from there. You don't want to build too many layers because it will become more difficult to hammer through multiple layers of tin. Continue until you have covered all intended surface areas. You do not have to make all pieces line up flush with the edges of your object if you want to leave some wood showing around the perimeter. Do be sure there are no dangerously sharp edges exposed or sticking up.

✔ Gently hammer down the tin between the nails and at the edges to make everything uniformly flat.

# garden art

Pssssst! Come closer; I have a secret for you. The key to creating great garden art is ... owning your very own rivet gun. Put this down on your next birthday list if you don't have one already. (See our gift ideas on page 27.) You'll have fun creating whimsical creatures to protect your vegetable garden. You'll use the same techniques as for tin art, with a few twists.

—Sarah

## Ready, set...

• A screen door brace is a metal rod with a flange at the end that reinforces a screen door to prevent it from twisting. These are available at hardware and home stores. If you don't know what a screen door brace is, walk confidently up to a store clerk and ask for one anyway. It will make this project a whole lot easier.

### WHAT YOU'LL NEED
- decorative tins
- tin snips
- screen door brace
- rivet gun and rivets
- hammer and nail

## Making your garden art

✔ Find an existing design on a piece of tin and cut it out, or create your own design from scrap pieces. Think in terms of creating a piece with separate parts to add intrigue to your garden creation. If you wish, design your creature to allow some appendages (wings, legs, antennae) to move.

✔ Lay everything out to prepare for assembly. Decide how best to attach your pieces together at two points corresponding to the holes in the door brace. Hammer holes through the tin with a nail at each point.

✔ Rev up that rivet gun and assemble your creature. If you want some parts to move, slip a few pieces of paper between the pieces of tin and fasten your rivet. When you pull out the pieces of paper, there will be enough space to allow easy movement.

✔ Attach your art piece to the screen door stretcher via the holes at one end. Stick the other end into the dirt, stand back, and revel in your creation.

# Fimo salt and pepper shakers

Nancy Mednick is a Seattle artist who runs an organization called Heart and Soul, going into local hospitals to work with patients on art projects. Through her years of presenting small projects at the sides of hospital beds, she has developed a treasure trove of easy-yet-satisfying craft ideas. These salt and pepper shakers are a good example. According to Nancy, the inspiration came from a pair of shakers that her sister bought for her in New York. Nancy looked at them and said, "Hmmmmmm, I could make those." You know the feeling.

This project has become one of my group's favorites on our getaway weekends. We've been making them for six years now and still keep coming up with new variations.

—Christine

## Ready, set...

• I buy glass salt-and-pepper shakers by the box (forty-eight pairs!) so I always have a set ready to give as a gift. My friends appreciate this.

• Which type of polymer clay to use? To each her own. Sculpey is a little less stiff and, for some, easier to work with—but I prefer FIMO.

• Decide on a theme for your shakers. Some options: pseudo-Wedgwood, polka dot, farm scenes, ocean scenes with fish and seaweed and black-and-white designs.

**WHAT YOU'LL NEED**
• restaurant glass salt and pepper shakers from a restaurant supply store
• polymer clay: FIMO or Sculpey
• small rolling pin or smooth drinking glass
• craft knife
• glossy varnish and brush

## Making your shakers

✔ Slice off one of the sections of clay. Using a rolling pin or glass, roll it out to about ⅛" (3mm) thick. You want the flattened clay to be roughly about as big as the palm of your hand.

✔ Unscrew the shaker's lid. Place the piece of flattened clay onto the shaker and, using your fingers, spread it over the entire glass surface. Cut off any excess clay just below the threads at the top of the shaker so that the lid will screw back on easily. One section of clay should be enough, but if you need more, cut a small piece and add it to the clay already on the shaker. It will get easier to work the longer you work with it, so keep smoothing the clay with your fingertips until you have a smooth surface on all sides.

✔ Cut, roll, twist and punch small pieces of clay to create your design. Add these to the base clay, pushing them on firmly enough to attach.

✔ When you are finished adorning both shakers, place them—still without the metal tops—in a cool oven (directly on the racks or on a cookie sheet). Cook for twenty minutes at 250° F (121° C) and remove the shakers from the oven. Use an oven thermometer to check the temperature so they don't burn.

✔ When they are completely cool, cover with a glossy varnish to add a protective shine to your tabletop masterpieces.

Ambition Scale

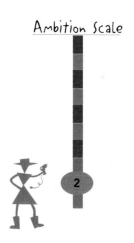

2

# Midas-touch box

Some years ago I read in the newspaper that Martha Stewart was visiting Seattle to demonstrate pumpkin gilding to members of the Junior League. No doubt, a gilded pumpkin must be a beautiful thing to behold, but it struck me as just the wrong thing to do to any self-respecting gourd. Since then, I've discovered gold leaf and its companions, silver leaf and copper leaf. Now I look at every object with a metallic gleam in my eye: How would it look ...? I have even gold-leafed rocks to use as paperweights. But I still don't think I'd ever gold-leaf a pumpkin. Perhaps a lily...

—Kitty

## Ready, set...

• I'm partial to copper leafing, so the examples shown here are in copper, but you can choose any metal leaf or experiment combining them.

• If you want some color to show through the cracks, cover the box with a coat of paint (dark reds, greens, blues and purples work well) and allow to dry thoroughly before leafing.

• Before handling the metallic leaf, wash your hands well and dry them thoroughly. Traditionally, metallic leaf is handled with a special brush (for applying gold to museum art frames, for example), but you can use your hands for a craft project such as this.

## Making your box

✔ First, line the interior of your box with decorative paper. I use Sunday newspaper comics to provide a fun contrast to the box's luxurious exterior. Maps, wrapping paper and origami paper are other options. Cut pieces of paper to size, use a brush to apply a light coat of white glue, and apply. If you want to avoid any chance of wrinkling, use spray adhesive.

✔ Use a small paintbrush or foam brush to apply an even layer of sizing over the entire outside of the box except for the bottom. The sizing will look white and milky. Leave this for an hour or so until you can no longer see the milky finish. The box will now be tacky to the touch.

✔ Open the packet of metallic leaf, reach in and pull out a piece of tissue paper with leaf on top. Slide the leaf off the tissue paper—careful now, don't sneeze—and lay it onto a surface of the box. For a smooth finish, lay the leaf on as flat as possible and lightly smooth it onto the box with the soft brush. Don't worry if it wrinkles or cracks appear in the process; you can always smooth them out and add more pieces to get the desired finish. Or, if you want color to show through some cracks, lay the leaf down in a deliberately sloppy manner.

✔ Continue covering surfaces of the box with sheets of leaf. If you miss spots between sheets, you can add more adhesive, tear off pieces of leaf, and stick them down in these areas.

Ambition Scale

3

✔ When the box and lid are covered, use your soft brush or your fingers to rub off all the excess bits of leaf. Push dangling bits down onto gaps or remove them to create gaps for the paint to show through. Keep brushing and blowing off flyaway bits until you have a nice, smooth gold surface.

✔ Add a coat of sealant, if you wish, but this isn't necessary. Decorate the box or leave it alone—either way, it makes a beautiful container to keep or use as a gift box.

# Cocktail-napkin plate

Two dear friends have shown me the far-ranging applications of this technique. Once I started, I couldn't stop. There are so many napkin designs to work with! Because of the multiple coats of polyurethane this requires, you'll only be able to assemble and give one or two coats to a plate in a sitting. Then give the final coats later. Still, this makes a fun project with friends when everyone brings a package of napkins to share.

—Anne

## Ready, set...

• Purchase your plates from a secondhand store. They should be smooth on the underside but can have etched or contoured top surfaces.

• Collect napkins wherever cocktails are served.

• Make certain that you use water-based, NOT oil-based, polyurethane. Work in an area with good ventilation. This project is simple but requires several days to complete due to the multiple applications of polyurethane.

• If you make a mistake when crafting your plate, you can soak it in warm water, peel off the paper, and start over.

• When finished, the plates should not be soaked in water or placed in the dish-washer; instead, they can be wiped clean with a damp cloth.

**WHAT YOU'LL NEED**
• clear glass plates
• tissue paper or paper napkins with eye-catching designs
• water-based polyurethane (glossy or clear)
• ½" (1cm) paintbrush
• craft knife

## Making your plate

✔ Spread out newspaper across your workspace. Stir the polyurethane well.

✔ Select the napkin(s) and/or tissue paper you want to work with. If you choose a paper napkin, peel away and discard all of the white, underside layers of the printed napkin. Check to see that your napkin or tissue paper will completely cover the underside of your selected plate.

✔ Restir the polyurethane a final time. With smooth, even strokes, apply a thin coat of polyurethane to the underside of the plate. Center the plate over your tissue paper or paper napkin and set it down; immediately flip the plate over and gently pat down all bubbles and smooth out all creases to even out and seal the paper. If the paper rips, soak your plate in water and peel off the paper; then dry off your plate and start over, this time with a gentler touch. With a little practice, you'll learn how to manipulate the wet paper.

✔ Allow your plate to dry completely (one to two hours or more). Apply a second, thin coat of polyurethane over all paper on the underside of the plate. Allow this coat to dry, and repeat the process another three or four times.

✔ When the plate has completely dried, take a single-edge razor or craft knife to trim the paper along the rim of the plate.

✔ Apply a final, thin coat of polyurethane, being careful to seal the edges of the paper and plate.

✔ VARIATION I: These plates can feature layers of different papers, pressed flowers, photos, stamps and acrylic paints. If you choose to create a collaged look,

think backwards. Adhere items to the underside of your plate as you'd want to see them from the top. For example, apply polyurethane to the front of a photo, pressed flowers or stamps, and press them onto the underside of your plate. When they dry, use acrylic paints to create decorative borders or background areas. After the paint dries, apply polyurethane to the underside of the plate, and pat down the final layer of tissue paper or a paper napkin. Apply additional coats of polyurethane as described above.

✔ VARIATION II: You can use this technique on cake plates, switch plates, lampshades, trays and boxes to create a vintage or a whimsical look. Bold experimentation often produces the best results.

Ambition Scale

# Some group endeavors

Obviously, nearly any project can be done with a group en masse. But some projects just seem meant for the overall group dynamic, either because of the mess factor (if you're making this much mess for yourself, you may as well make it for others) or because of the simplicity, or because of the fun. Here are a few ideas for projects we have enjoyed together. You can find detailed instructions for these at any number of crafting Web sites.

## Bath salts

Once you make your own bath salts, you'll never buy them again; it's so easy! Just mix epsom salts with some baking soda and drops of one or more essential oils, and you're done. Then you can spend the rest of the evening decorating the containers.

## Fun soap

Provide blocks of glycerine soap, scents and a kitchen for an afternoon or evening. Have your friends bring various molds and unexpected objects to embed inside the soaps. TIP: Use the freezer for solidifying the soap more quickly. One Christmas we made dozens and dozens of bars with coconut "snow" floating around a tiny toy snowman.

## Garden pavers

This is a fun group project for the summer months when it stays light late and you can work outside and enjoy the evening. People bring broken dishware and found objects from around the house and have a good time playing with the "mud." We use heavy-duty plastic mesh trays, either rectangular or square, given out by nurseries, as molds. Then we line them with foil, mix up a batch of Quick Crete mortar mix, and pour it in. Swirl some acrylic paints into the very top layer of concrete around the embedded objects for some color.

## Flavored vinegars

Choose your base vinegar to compliment the flavoring ingredients you're using. Apple cider vinegar goes well with fruits; white distilled vinegar pairs with most herbs; wine vinegar works with stronger herbs such as garlic and tarragon and rice vinegar is good for Asian flavors. Assemble a range of flavoring ingredients to allow everyone to customize. These can include fresh herbs, edible flower petals, spices, fruits and garlic cloves.

## Curry mix

Make your own spice mixes—curry (dried red chiles, coriander seeds, mustard seeds, black peppercorns, fenugreek seeds, ground ginger and ground turmeric) or garam masala (cumin, coriander seeds, cardamom, black peppercorns, cloves, mace, bay leaf and cinnamon), for example.

## Party poppers

Save your empty toilet paper tubes all year and make these favors, also known as Christmas crackers, for the holidays. These are traditional accompaniments to various British celebrations and date from Victorian times. You fill the tubes with treats (confetti, candies, a paper crown, a bell necklace strung on a ribbon), tape a small charge in each and wrap them in tissue paper.

## Papier mâché pets

Have everyone mold the armatures for their stationary pets at home, and then transport them to a gathering where you all bring them to life with papier mâché. Margaret made the examples shown here: Speedo, the yellow lab (so named because he moves so fast he appears to be standing still all the time), was a present to a friend who claimed he wanted a dog, and Smoke the cat came to life as a memorial to her son's beloved pet, who disappeared one night and never returned.

# Recommended resources

## Web sites

### Archie McPhee
In addition to carrying items you can't believe you've lived without—the Freud action figure, the pig catapult and the punching nun puppet, to name a few—Archie carries an array of plastic figures for assemblage projects and printed oddities for collages. Order the catalog; it's too funny to miss.
www.mcphee.com

### Beading with Eden
Beading patterns
www.rockfront.com

### Beadworks
Beading supplies
www.beadworks.com

### Bedrock Industries
100 percent recycled glass for any number of projects; they offer faux sea glass (tumbled shards of recycled bottles) in a range of rich colors.
www.bedrockindustries.com

### Button Bug
Antique and collectable buttons
www.iserv.net/~dbuttons

### Forcefield
Surplus ceramic and rare earth magnets and other products sold wholesale/retail for science projects, hobbies, industrial uses or just plain fun.
www.wondermagnet.com

### fridgedoor
Check out this site for great magnet ideas and supplies for making them.
www.fridgedoor.com

### Global Beads
Beads, African art and gifts
www.globalbeads.com

### Grafix
Fun, funky art supplies including funky films, funky three-dimensional film, funky tape and funky fur; and did we mention faux film and frisket film? Check out the "Incredible Art Products" category.
www.grafixarts.com

### Impress
Rubber stamps
www.impressrubberstamps.com

### The Lamp Shop
Download or request a catalog to find out about lamp-making parts you never knew you couldn't live without.
www.lampshop.com

### Lucky Squirrel
Artist's grade shrink plastic; go to the artist's gallery to see the amazing possibilities.
www.luckysquirrel.com

### Mendel's
Art supplies, stationery and "far-out fabrics"; get your fake fur here.
www.mendels.com

### National Artcraft
Another good craft site, with a selection of lamp-making supplies.
www.nationalartcraft.com

### NASCO
This site started as a supply house for science teachers but you should see it now! Here's your source for a range of art materials and petri dishes.
www.nascofa.com

### Paper Candy
A line of fun and unusual rubber stamping supplies.
www.papercandy.com

### Sanibel Seashell Industries
The treasures of the ocean at your fingertips—over 10,000 different shells; they also sell sea glass.
www.seashells.com

ShrinkyDinks
Supplies for making small versions of favorite pictures for shrines, jewelry and other projects.
www.shrinkydinks.com

3M Worldwide
The most durable and colorful tape for the spines of handmade books is Scotch Colored Plastic Tape (catalog #191). Check for the nearest supplier.
www.3m.com

TSI
This site (and their store in Seattle) is a jeweler's paradise of supplies.
www.tsijeweltools.com

What You Need to Know About Beadwork
A good section on beading patterns
www.beadwork.about.com

World of Charms
Charms for necklaces, bracelets anklets and anything else you can think of.
www.worldofcharms.com

Zettiology
More great rubber stamps
www.zettiology.com

# Books

The Art Doll Chronicles: A Collaborative Journey of Discovery
Catherine Moore
Stampington & Co., 2003

Beautiful Necessity: The Art and Meaning of Women's Altars
Kay Turner
Thames & Hudson, 1999

Collage for the Soul: Expressing Hopes and Dreams Through Art
Holly Harrison & Paula Grasdal
Rockport Publishers, 2003

Decorating with Mosaics
Deborah Schneebeli-Morrell
North Light Books, 1999

Home and Garden Metalcrafts
Jana Ewy
North Light Books, 2003

La Casa Loca: Latino Style Comes Home 45 Funky Craft Projects for Decorating & Entertaining
Kathy Cano-Murillo
Rockport Publishers, 2003

Making Journals by Hand
Jason Thompson
Rockport Publishers, 2000

Magic Lanterns: Creative Projects for Making and Decorating Lanterns for Indoors and Out
Mary Maguire
North Light Books, 2002

Making Shadow Boxes and Shrines
Kathy Cano-Murillo
Rockport Publishers, 2002

Pebble Mosaics: Step-by-Step Projects for Inside and Out
Ann Frith
David & Charles, 2002

# Index

## Acknowledgments

Thank you to the wonderfully inventive and end-lessly supportive women in our groups: Women Who Do Things with Their Hands (Charlotte Beall, Sarah Brace, Libs Schlater, Florence Moravia, Cynthia Livak, Meg Goldman, Sarah Robertson-Palmer, Kay Kowanko, Lisa Greenberg, Luzita Roll, Marilyn Zucker, Sandra Marulanda, Catherine Karr and Carla Orlando) and Women Who Run with Glue Guns (Margaret Foster, Lisa Irwin, Jane Jeszeck, Lea Johnson, Maryann Jordan, Rita O'Boyle, Julie O'Brien, Pamela Rhoads, Robyn Ricks, Dana Servheen, Lynn Tchobanoglous, Anne Tillery and Beth Young).

And special thanks to those group members and friends who contributed to the book in myriad won-derful ways: Will Anderson, Charlotte Beall, Lisa Crabtree, Margaret Foster, Terry Frankel, Phyl Harmon, Camille Horne, Lisa Irwin, Leslie Jacobs, Kay Kowanko, Cynthia Livak, Nancy Mednick, Anne Mulherkar, Rita O'Boyle, Sarah Robertson-Palmer, Wendy Smith-Novick, Lynn Tchobanoglous, Anne Tillery and Beth Young.

For their help in creating the section, "Women Uniting in Creativity" (pages 18-20) we extend our thanks to: Emily Arfin (El Quetzal), Linda Chalmers (Oxfam), Juanita Fox (10,000 Villages), Paola Gianturco and Toby Tuttle, authors of *In Her Hands: Craftswomen Changing the World*, Judith Haden (Casita), Dick Meyer (Traditions and Fair Trade Federation) and Daniel Salcedo (PEOPLink).

PROJECT CREDITS
Charlotte Beall: pages 34-35
Lisa Crabtree: page 110
Margaret Foster: pages 7-9, 82-83, 139
Terry Frankel: pages 5, 36-37
Kitty Harmon: pages 32, 33, 35, 36-37, 46-47, 50-51, 60-61, 64-65, 66-67, 70, 72-73, 74-75, 79, 92, 94-95, 100-101, 104-105, 107, 109, 111, 112-113, 114-115, 118-119, 121, 134-135, 138, 139
Phyl Harmon: pages 107-109
Camille Horne: pages 90-91
Lisa Irwin: pages 71, 72-73, 86-87, 93, 121
Jane Jeszeck: pages 68-69
Kay Kowanko: pages 100-101
Cynthia Livak: pages 40-41, 58-59
Anne Mulherkar: pages 136-137
Sarah Robertson-Palmer: pages 2, 54-55, 126-127, 128-129, 130-131
Christine Stickler: pages 36-37, 38, 42-43, 48-49, 52-53, 56-57, 78-81, 84-85, 96-97, 98-99, 106-107, 120-121, 122-123, 124-125, 127, 132-133
Lynn Tchobanoglous: pages 34-35, 39, 71, 120-121

PHOTO CREDITS
Will Anderson: page 81
Jim Fagiolo: pages 5, 7, 8, 9, 28, 29, 32, 33, 34, 35, 36 (top), 37, 39, 40, 41, 42, 44-45, 46, 47, 49, 50 (bottom), 51 (two at right), 52, 53, 55, 60, 61, 62-63, 71, 76-77, 79, 83, 84, 85, 88-89, 90, 91, 93, 97, 100, 102-103, 106, 111, 116-117, 120 (lower right), 121, 122, 125, 133, 134
Paola Gianturco/Toby Tuttle: page 18 (upper right)
Judith Haden: page 19
Kitty Harmon: pages 15, 16, 30-31, 36 (bottom), 50 (top), 51 (upper left), 64, 65, 66, 67, 68, 69, 71, 72, 73, 74, 75, 86, 87, 92, 94, 95, 98, 99, 104, 105, 107, 108, 109, 112, 113, 114, 115, 118, 119, 130, 132, 138, 139
Anne Mulherkar: 136, 137
Sarah Robertson-Palmer: pages 2, 128, 129, 130
Christine Stickler: pages 6, 11, 12, 13, 26-27, 38, 48, 56, 57, 58, 59, 96, 101 (lower left), 110, 120 (upper right), 123, 126, 127
Sarah Sanford: page 17
Chris Viola: page 23

# Get Creative with North Light Books!

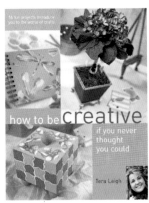

Let Tera Leigh act as your personal craft guide and motivator. She'll help you discover just how creative you really are. You'll explore eight exciting crafts through 16 fun, fabulous projects, including rubber stamping, bookmaking, papermaking, collage, decorative painting and more.
**ISBN 1-58180-293-5, paperback, 128 pages, #32170-K**

Let Mary Jo McGraw, renowned rubber stamp artist and card maker, show you how to create handmade cards that capture the look and feel of antiques and heirlooms. You'll create 23 gorgeous cards using easy-to-find heirloom papers, old family photos and ephemera.
**ISBN 1-58180-413-X, paperback, 128 pages, #32583-K**

You can create gorgeous home decor and garden art using today's new, craft-friendly metals, meshes and wire. You'll find 15 projects, ranging from lamps to picture frames. Most can be completed in an afternoon!
**ISBN 1-58180-330-3, paperback, 96 pages, #32296-K**

Collage is the perfect medium to help you unleash your creative potential. There are no rules or mistakes, and your supplies are simple. Learn how to master 15 favorite collage techniques, including image transfer, working with beeswax and antiquing found objects.
**ISBN 1-58180-343-5, paperback, 128 pages, #32313-K**

Now you can combine the self-expressive qualities of rubber stamping with the elegance of jewelry-making. It's easier than you think! Sharilyn Miller provides all of the tips and techniques you need in 20 exciting wearable art projects.
**ISBN 1-58180-384-2, paperback, 128 pages, #32415-K**

Celebrate every season with a handmade wreath! America's Flower Man Dale Rohman shows you how to add elegance and personality to any room, door or occasion. These 20 fantastic wreath and garland projects are guaranteed to elicit "ooh"s and "ah"s.
**ISBN 1-58180-289-7, paperback, 128 pages, #32165-K**

These and other fine North Light Titles are available from your local art & craft retailer, bookstore, online supplier or by calling 1-800-448-0915.